BREAKING FREE

The Journey of a Reluctant Healer

By

Julie Ann Bradley

CREDITS

UK Editor: Mel Ledgard

US Editor: Jeff Hutner, newparadigmdigest.com

Cover design: Bryan Ledgard, bryanledgard.com

Layout & Wordpress site: Wayne Marshall, kaizen-marketing.com

Publicity: Custom PR Ltd, UK

First published in 2012 in the United States of America

ISBN-13: 978-1478280736
ISBN-10: 1478280735

DEDICATION

This book is dedicated in celebration of our multi-dimensionality.

Julie Ann Bradley

ACKNOWLEDGEMENTS

With love and gratitude to my loving guides in the
higher dimensions: without you there would be no book
at all. Thank you for allowing me to be your channel, my
beloved teachers.

To my dearest friend and Earth guide, Jeff Hutner. I
hold you in my heart for your unconditional acceptance,
support, loving guidance and wisdom. You have been
instrumental in bringing this book into the world.
Words cannot express my gratitude to you and your own
work. You are a gift to humanity and the Earth. To my
loving Earth guide Pat, thank you for walking every step
of the way with me. You have been my unwavering
support throughout this epic journey, selflessly putting
yourself aside on too many occasions to mention. The
love I feel for you is beyond it all.

Mum Sheila and Grandma Julia, I am forever
blessed for the experience you gave me on this physical
plane. I love you with all my heart and look forward to
our meeting again out of the Illusion. The brightest
lights ever, my beautiful children Ashley and Stacey, you
are my inspiration and I am ever indebted to you for

allowing me the freedom to pursue my mission. I love you both with all my heart.

In loving memory of Les, the father of my children. Your presence is ever close; thank you for continuing to watch over them.

My little Star boy, Blake, you are a shining example of the new human being. Nana loves you and you are a blessing to the new Earth. To my brother and sisters who may not fully understand my chosen path but always provided loving support throughout the years, love always.

Jill, you are the quiet Angel, thank you for your constant support and unconditional love. You have always believed in me and everything I do. My Tibetan soul sister Sarjana, in love and gratitude to who you are, a pure healing channel of love. Thank you for being in my life. Beloveds Mel and Bryan Ledgard, many blessings to you both for your practical support in helping get this book into print with your editing and design work. Gwen, my dear friend and soul sister: I am honoured to be part of your circle, you beautiful human being. May we continue to share time together on your beloved Isle of Anglesey, the Mother Isle that has enriched and inspired my work since the day I stepped onto her some 30 years ago. Roger and Dorothy, hidden treasures, holding the frequency of Love on Orsedd Isaf. You have selflessly assisted so many beings who have crossed your path and my love for you both is beyond words. And to the rest of my wonderful family and friends who have supported me in this quest, thanks to each of you.

Above all, my deepest love and thanks to my patient, loving partner James, who has been ever close in the process of writing this book. You are my greatest mirror and you have my heart.

Bob, you were a wise old chief and Rosie, you kept me still while I completed this book.

- Julie

FOREWORD

Healing is an art and, like every other profession, there are a small number of practitioners that stand out as extraordinary. Perhaps it's as little as 1/10th of 1% or less but whatever the number, you know them when you are in their presence. You feel different around them. They exude an air of confidence without ego or boasting. In other words, they are just being themselves. They are simply and authentically living their passion.

These individuals do not always come to their profession easily. Some come kicking and screaming and trying as best they can to avoid living their destined calling. But after many tries, they may finally surrender and become the person they were meant to be and in the process can often help many others to follow their soul's calling.

Julie Ann Bradley is one of those people and from all accounts an extraordinary healer. On the pages of this intimate portrait, Julie shares the many hills and valleys of her life. The result is a look into the heart and soul of a gifted healer who has positively impacted the lives of hundreds of clients in the UK and US.

Perhaps you will have an opportunity to work with Julie one day but if you never meet her in person, thanks to her book, you will understand her path and that of so many like her. Julie was one of the resistors but is now a conductor of the healing energy of universal love she so generously shares with her clients.

The world needs more like her. Perhaps this book will encourage others to follow in her footsteps and live their soul's healing calling no matter the profession.

Jeff Hutner, Editor, New Paradigm Digest

Chapters

Introduction 1

Early Days 3

Mother Ship.. 10

Family Changes 12

Manifestations... 20

School, Boys and Beyond 23

Settling Down... 30

Finding Healing... 35

From Washington D.C. to Cornwall 40

Lessons 45

Changes 48

Magical Anglesey.. 52

Friendship with a Druid.. 56

Trials in Thailand 60

Moving On.. 64

Egypt Calling 67

John of God 70

Taking on Teaching... 79

Energetic Blood 83

The Gateway... 86

Australia 90

The Indian Connection 92

Trip to LA 98

Spirit Surgery 102

Mum 105

Star Beings.. 108

Luminaries 112

Alone Again 117

Sedona 120

Love 127

Walking Away 132

Illness and Peace.................................... 136

In the Stars.. 142

Postscript : Three Healing Stories........................... 145
    Cosmic Brain Surgery
    A Need to Share
    Becoming the Temple of the Heart: An
    Extraordinary Healer

Photos.. 158

INTRODUCTION

This is the moment where I tell you that cosmic beings performed brain surgery in my cottage one Monday afternoon. I believe this with absolute conviction. If someone had asked me about the possibility of such an occurrence, even just the day before, I would have laughed myself silly. But here's me now, still almost unbelieving, but hand on heart, saying that cosmic brain surgery is what took place that day and this is how it happened...

    – Jane Hodson

Over the course of my life journey, I have encountered extraordinary people and witnessed events that have convinced me that our minds play a pivotal role in creating our reality.

This conclusion forms the basis of a new paradigm which states that the universe is not solid and material but is made up of energy and that our lives are created by our consciousness.

In telling my story from the perspective of an ordinary person, my goal is to let others who may doubt their abilities know that, in truth, we are all extraordinary.

I moved from being a reluctant healer to accepting my calling, ultimately stepping into my destiny that is the journey each of us is on.

I have changed the identities of some people to protect their privacy.

EARLY DAYS

Our birth is but a sleep and a forgetting: The Soul that rises with us, our life's Star, Hath had elsewhere its setting, And cometh from afar.
    – William Wordsworth

I have always felt that I dropped out of the cosmos. I never felt like Earth was my first planet. Mum said I was a strange and moody kid with a grasshopper mind.

I intuitively understood the ride I was in for. People's habits seemed very strange to me. They sat in a large building called a church every Sunday, prayed to what they told me was God and then, when they came away from that building, they were not kind to each other. I didn't get it. It was as if God only showed up in their lives once a week.

My knees really hurt from kneeling on wooden planks for what seemed like hours. What I felt most drawn to in that church were the beautiful stained glass windows that mesmerized me. I loved them though they didn't help with the pain in my knees. It seemed to me that if a God existed, He or She would surely let us all discover and experience that spirit in our own time and way. Furthermore, I was much more comfortable talking with Him or Her lying on my bed or in the grass.

I also felt a special connection with the stars. They connected me with another time and space, giving me a sense of where I had really come from, and what I strongly felt was my true home.

I was three years old when my Mum, Sheila, met her husband Jack. She was so happy to be able to take the two of us to what she hoped would be a better life away from my Grandma's watchful eye. I had been conceived 'out of wedlock'. Mum had fallen head-over-heels for the man she worked for and he did all the right things to woo her. It lasted six months until she informed him that I was on the way. He was married, and that was that. History had repeated itself and my Mum had done the unthinkable and followed in Grandma's footsteps. She too had her daughter Winnie out of wedlock.

I arrived on the 19th of November 1960. We lived with my Grandma, Julia Ann Bradley, for whom I was named. In those days it was a terrible shame to be unmarried and pregnant so I can't begin to imagine how it was for Grandma in the 20's. After the initial shock and shouting calmed down, the reality of the situation set in. Grandma lived in a one-bedroom flat and Mum's sisters and brothers, who were all married and had their own children, didn't have a spare room either.

Grandma saw no other choice and sent my Mum to a Manchester convent that accepted unmarried pregnant women. Many of them stayed there for years.

The nuns were very strict and when Grandma came to visit, my heavily pregnant Mum was on all fours scrubbing the floors – her daily task since arriving a month earlier. Maybe they thought the punishment would teach the women a lesson. Grandma went home and found a two-bedroom house. Mum was once again in the fold.

The three of us lived together in a small terraced house in Portwood, not far from our town centre in Stockport. As money was very scarce, Mum had to return to work as soon as she was well enough. Her job? Cleaning out railway carriages at Edgeley train station. Grandma took care of me during the day. Mum was so exhausted from her daytime work that on retiring at night she would put me into bed beside her. It was her way of keeping me close because she missed me so much. Quite often she would wake up in the early hours of the morning to find I had fallen out onto the oilcloth floor and rolled underneath the old wooden bed. I would quickly be grabbed by my flannel nightie, almost frozen to death, and pulled back into bed.

One day, she returned home from work to find no sign of me and asked her mother where I was. A shocked Grandma realised she had taken me to the shops in my pram and totally forgotten me. Running to the shops, Mum found me in the care of the local butcher who kept me safe after Grandma bought her tripe and left me behind. After that, I was put into full-time nursery care at Saint Paul's School. My Auntie Kath, who made the school meals there, would drop me off and pick me up each day.

Our Victorian terraced house had many of its original features, including fireplaces in both the upstairs and downstairs rooms. I loved to watch the flames die down while falling into slumber. On one occasion, I stumbled out of bed in search of the potty and stepped straight onto the red-hot poker that had fallen out of its holder. The pain was intense and I clearly remember the pandemonium it caused. Even at that young age, I wondered why Grandma thought it best to immerse my whole foot into a bag of flour, which only worsened the pain. Surely cold water would have done the trick.

One of the tasks Grandma gave me was cream-stoning the front doorstep, the sign of a good clean house in those days. I much preferred popping the warm tar bubbles that swelled between the cobblestones that lined the roads. It had to be a scorching hot day for that though, and usually led to a good hiding for coming home covered in the stuff.

The parish priest would call regularly, which I thought was a very kind thing to do until I discovered that he came to ask for money. Unfortunately for him, neither Grandma nor Mum had any to spare. Some days we hid under the stairs to avoid having to open the door for him, which left them both riddled with guilt. It was all very puzzling to me as I thought it should have been the other way around, Mum and Grandma asking him for help.

I would have been about two years old when I received my first trike. It was big, red, and very shiny. I remember jumping up and down with excitement at the very sight of it. It took me no time at all to master riding it and off I went like a Tasmanian devil. Grandma would look out into the cobbled street to check on me, only to find I had 'bombed it off' several streets away in a bid for escape. I think I might have been trying to head back to my stars.

I must have been a real handful, as quite often I would be dragged off to the local home for naughty children. Mum said I was so stubborn that I would never take no for an answer. I would cry and beg all the way up to the threatening gates of what looked like the Addams Family house. However, I discovered later that this building was no home of correction, but the local gas works. It accomplished the task of shutting me up for a while though.

Soon after my third birthday, my Mum met Jack, an Irishman who worked at Needham's Foundry at the end of our street. Needham's made the iron grid coverings that lined the cobbled streets across the country. Within a short time, they were married at Saint Bernadette's church – another of the large buildings that played a part in my life. I remember feeling very uncomfortable in the white puffed-up dress and basin-shaped bonnet they had bought me. I just wanted to get back to playing outdoors on my bike. They found a house not too far away from Grandma. It was my Mum's first house and I had never seen her so happy. Soon after, we discovered that Jack liked to drink. A lot.

Compared to Grandma's, the house was huge. It had three bedrooms and I was allowed to pick my own room. I was really excited when I first opened the door to the little six-foot by seven-foot box room and saw the spaceship wallpaper and a star-covered ceiling. Perfect! I felt like I was at home.

Mum always said she always knew where to find me. I would be lying on my bed staring at the stars while listening to my first and only record, the one that she had bought me to go with my new record player. It was Telstar by The Tornados. It made me feel happy and sad at the same time and I would play it over and over again until I fell asleep.

I loved the fields around our house and could often be found there too, lying among the ferns and looking up at the sky. I had my first taste of freedom living in that house. I had never seen so much green grass before. It was a little glimpse of heaven.

Times were tough and money was scarce in the few years we lived there. Mum had three more children: my two sisters Denise and Ann and, finally, a long-awaited son, my brother John. Much of the money Jack earned at the foundry went to fuel his sessions at the pub and it became normal for all of us to be hungry and frightened. The nights were filled with the sound of Mum and Jack screaming at each other often ending with physical fights. On my return from school, I would often find Mum lying on the sofa with a migraine.

I quickly learned to cook and clean for us as the bouts became more frequent. Mum was simply overwhelmed by trying to cope with four young kids and an abusive husband. I began to dread the days ahead and would always be in trouble at school for not concentrating.

Each Friday, Jack would pick up his pay packet and head straight for the pub. My mother put my younger siblings in her bed – her way of trying to protect them from his explosive drunken behavior. She would keep me with her, another way to try to diffuse his violence.

One night she saw him coming down the road with several other men carrying crates of beer. We locked the door but they used the crate as a battering ram and she was forced to open it. Jack wanted to show off his children to his friends. They all stamped upstairs and woke my sisters and brother. Having frightened them half to death and left them crying, Jack turned his attention to me, not to show me off, but to torment my mother's 'little English bastard', as he always called me. He ranted and raved at the two of us, calling me an ugly child who was not his. Mother felt powerless to stand up to him. Eventually, after the bottles were empty, peace would return as Jack slipped into his usual drunken stupor. The only way I was able to cope with all this was to connect with my stars.

MOTHER SHIP

"Set your course by the stars, not by the lights of every passing ship."
 – Omar N Bradley

It was a cold November night before my sixth birthday. My Mum, Auntie Kath and I were taking the short walk from our house back to hers. We came from quite a large and close-knit Catholic family. Grandma had seven children but I only knew six of them: Mum, three sisters and two brothers. The eldest sister, Winnie, had died of consumption (tuberculosis) at the age of 24. Grandma said I was Winnie come back to life. I guess she believed in reincarnation

 I can remember having to almost run to keep up with them as they hurried to escape the biting wind. As usual, I was in my own world, staring up at the stars in the heavenly night sky and being careful not to trip. The stars were my one constant comfort in what was a mad, chaotic world and as always, I looked forward to the hot malt drink my Auntie gave me when I visited.

We were approaching the Labour Club, where the family often met to have a drink. They were all happy when they spent time in that particular building, but there were no beautiful colored windows there for me.

When I first saw it, I pulled on my Mum's hand, shouting to stop and look up. We stopped in our tracks and I heard Mum say, "Oh my God, Kath, can you see what I see?" For some reason, I was very comfortable with the sight of the spaceship that seemed to have appeared out of nowhere. It was massive, disc-shaped, and pulsating with the very colors that seemed to haunt me. I loved it! Within seconds, it shot off vertically into the starry sky. I wildly hoped the ship had come to rescue me from my unhappy life.

I felt as if my body was tingling from head to toe, and that feeling has returned at important times throughout my life. My Mum and Auntie couldn't believe what they had seen and the event was the topic of conversation that night and for years after.

For me, that was the start of my relationship with what I knew by instinct to be my true family, my 'imaginary friends' – beings from the stars – and I wanted to keep the image I had seen that night in my mind and heart forever. What was to follow over the next 47 years was what can only be described as one big ride – and not the happy type that you take at the funfair.

Family Changes

"When it gets dark enough you can see the stars."
– Persian folk saying

Jack and Mum's fights got worse. However, she was allowed to go out once a week with my older cousin who lived near by. She seemed much happier on returning, but I wasn't. Jack never took to the "ugly little kid" and began locking me in the wardrobe while he and my brother and sisters watched TV. He thought this would stop my Mum from going out. It didn't work. Mum had found her escape.

Sometime later, Mum announced she'd met Jerry, a policeman in the Criminal Investigation Department. He was originally from Berkshire, had come north to work on the infamous Moors Murders case and decided to stay. Jerry and Mum had fallen head over heels in love and informed me that we were all – barring Jack of course – going to move to a new house together. Brilliant!

At last I could feel safe and dearly hoped that I would not have to take any more trips to big buildings where once a week I was expected to sit in a dark box and tell my every action to the ghostly figure on the other side of the grill. I had nightmares leading up to confession day and spent hours wondering if the priest would one day say it was my time to visit the place called Hell that he often mentioned. At least I got to sit down in that wooden box. I didn't know which was worse, red raw knees from the wooden kneeler or blinding headaches from trying to recall every sin I had committed in between walking to school and returning home each day.

The big day arrived and off we all went while Jack was at work, taking our belongings with us. Mum did not leave Jack without however. He was left one plate, one knife and fork and his favorite pint glass for his Guinness. It was very disturbing to me. Was this normal? Did people really just up and walk away and not talk to each other about it first? Apparently. I can honestly say that I never once saw them sit and talk to each other in a civil manner. I would never understand that strange human thing called Love.

There was lots of excitement in the removal van as we made our escape and all was going well until we arrived at the 'new' house. They said it was all they could find given such a short time. It was another house, but this time a run-down two-up, two-down with a broken toilet at the end of the yard.

We four kids shared one back bedroom with a view of the outside toilet and Mum and Jerry had the front room, which at least didn't have a gaping hole in the ceiling. We got used to waking up with pigeons staring down at us along with gale-force winds coming through the hole. Oh well, I thought, maybe lots of people lived like this, as odd as it seemed.

Soon Mum and Jerry found the local pub across the road and it started all over again. When they went out, I would sit my brother and sisters and loved telling them faerie stories to keep them happy. At least I got my wish of not having to sit in the wooden box anymore, although I really missed those beautiful colored windows.

Years passed and I longed to know more about my father's identity and why he never visited me. My Mum would tell me I had his freckled nose and long fingers. I hung onto every word about him. Apparently he was an accomplished pianist, a Freemason, and rich. He owned a launderette that washed and ironed its patron's clothes. It was the first in our town and where my Mum had worked and been wooed by him. She told me they had both appeared in court in a custody battle for me when I was only a few months old. Apparently he and his wife, unable to have children themselves wanted to adopt me.

Grandma had put her foot down and said that she and Mum were going to keep me, no matter what. It made me feel a little better knowing that he did want me at one time. On one occasion Grandma marched me into his shop and said to him, "Say hello, this is your daughter!" I remember looking up at him across the high sales counter that I could barely see over. He smiled at me and said, "Hello Julie, do you want anything?" I stammered, "No, thank you" and ran out of the shop shaking and red-faced, and begged Grandma not to make me do that again. She told me he would come for me one day. I waited for him, but he never did.

Still, I always had my stars!

Once again we were on the move. Two more houses, both not far from the first house in Hillgate, and then a third move back near my Grandma in Brinnington. Through the years, she and I were always very close. She really believed I was her Winnie reincarnated. I would spend as much time as I could with her to escape the mayhem now going on between Mum and Jerry. My sisters and brother were growing up and, in between arguing and fighting among themselves, they took pleasure in tormenting the life out of me. I just didn't fit in.

I was very proud of my little bedroom and the few possessions I had managed to gather, mainly my precious books. My favorites were autobiographies I found at our local market in the second-hand bookstall. The first one I picked up was about Marilyn Monroe, formerly Norma Jean Baker. I completely lost myself reading her story. She was beautiful not only in her looks, but in the person she was behind the image that was projected onto her. Totally different in every way was the Moors Murders story.

I was intrigued to know how Myra Hindley, being a woman, could commit such acts of cruelty. What a world, full of such diversity! I remember thinking it was as if we were all actors on a stage and that one day we would all meet again and discover the real reasons we chose to play our parts. I read many books like these over the years and it helped me understand much of what I was experiencing.

Another of my hobbies was collecting bottles of nail polish in every conceivable color. I lined them up, dozens of them, on the windowsill where I could see them in their full glory. To brighten up the dull walls I cut pictures out of magazines and pasted them onto the wall facing my bed. The result seemed magical to me. I picked images of what I wanted to see instead of the grey streets and buildings I had to live in.

There were beautiful people and places I longed to visit, planets and my stars, flowers and dolphins swimming in the sea, and faeries and angels. It was like entering another world, a happier one full of love and joy. My Mum thought it was very clever of me. I would lie on my bed and dream I was in that world.

I loved to visit Grandma. She always had bread in the cupboard and it was tasty brown Hovis, not like in our house where one cheap loaf a day was rationed between the six of us. I loved walking with her to the off-license to pick up two bottles of Guinness that she said were medicinal. She would take the poker out of the fire and plunge it into the Guinness, believing the drink was full of iron and that the hot poker would increase its strength. I knew she would treat me to a bag of crisps and a bottle of Dandelion and Burdock. Talk about cupboard love!

We would sit up late at night and she never tired of answering my many questions about life. Her own had been very hard, bringing up seven children with little money. She only had herself to rely on since Grandad died in his early fifties from cancer. She said, "God is good, Julie. You will find out. He never gives you more than you can handle". I remember her words to this day. We always seem to find a way, no matter what we must deal with in life. It reminds me now of the saying that what doesn't kill you makes you stronger.

On one occasion, she told me a story. One night, while all her children were in bed asleep, she sensed something was wrong. To her horror she could smell smoke and quickly ran down the stairs. A fire had started, although she couldn't understand how. Amazingly, the fire had traveled along the bottom floor of the house in a straight line and then just stopped, directly before a picture of the Sacred Heart of Jesus that hung on the wall. She believed it to be a miracle, it being impossible for the flames to die down in such a way. She filled me with faith and taught me to trust that everything happens for a reason, even though it may not be apparent at the time.

When I was about nine, on several occasions while staying with her, I had strange out-of-body experiences. Half asleep, I sensed a crowd of presences trying to communicate with me. I wasn't scared at all. I felt myself expanding until I became nothing. These experiences became more frequent as time went on and I began to encourage these presences to talk to me. It became completely normal for them to show themselves to me whenever I wanted them to. I thought of them as my friends and that's exactly how they acted.

When I told Grandma she just accepted it and said she had never feared the dead folk, only the living. She was such a wise old lady, although it took me time to realize that. As Franklin D. Roosevelt reminded us, "there is nothing to fear but fear itself". Grandma never judged me and it was easy to share my experiences with her. As time went on, I found that I could travel anywhere in my mind and meet anyone I wanted. I thought it best not to confide this in anyone else for fear of ridicule.

Back at home one school morning I went downstairs and discovered a note from Jerry. It said he had left my Mum and was returning to his hometown in Berkshire. After seven years, he just walked away. Mum took to her bed for weeks. The shock almost killed her and she never really recovered. I did what I could but there was nothing that eased her unbearable emotional pain. I felt so bad for Mum, although I wasn't much bothered myself.

The previous Christmas, the fighting had reached new heights and we woke up to find that in a rage, Jerry had broken every one of our few toys. They were thrown about, some lying in the food strewn over the kitchen floor. The neighbors called the police and we were taken, somewhat traumatized, to my Uncle Bob's house not far away. The Wizard of Oz, was on their TV and it's forever associated in my memory with that awful day.

I used to stay home from school and look after my sisters and brother, get the shopping, and help make food for us until Mum could get back on her feet. After things settled down again, we eventually moved to an apartment. Mum began to drink a lot more and as I saw it, the drink was her friend. It helped her bury her past a little.

Later, Mum had a relationship with David, a complex man who would do his utmost to pretend that there was only the two of them in the home and that we kids didn't exist at all. He could completely ignore us and get into dark moods that lasted for days. We kept out of his way as much as possible which was easier for me, being the oldest and having a job by then. Mum tried to keep the peace but it didn't last very long before the fighting began again. The relationship only lasted a few years and they eventually separated. David died from a heart attack while driving a coach in France on a school trip.

MANIFESTATIONS

"Life and death are one thread, the same line viewed from different sides."
– Lao Tzu

I was always very popular and had many friends in the area to play with. We used to enjoy camping-out nights in the fields across from our house. I would take every opportunity I could to spend time under my stars. My Mum despaired and said that I had become a tomboy overnight. She never knew what was coming next with me or where I would end up. I just wanted adventure.

My friend Bernadette knew a woman on the next street who was looking for a babysitter. I eagerly offered my services without telling Mum, who would have forbidden the very idea. I went over to the house every Friday evening at 7 pm for three hours while my employers enjoyed a well-earned evening out at the end of the working week. One Friday, two of my friends sat with me for company. Towards the end of the evening, my employers had returned and we were all chatting about the movie they had seen at the cinema.

20

Suddenly the light fixture in the ceiling above our heads began swinging of its own accord, at first slowly and then quite aggressively. We all ran to one side of the room and huddled together in fear. It didn't stop, just kept on and on moving violently. 10pm arrived and I had to be getting home. If I wasn't back at my usual time, I was afraid my Mum would find out what I'd been doing. I plucked up the courage to run to the living room door but it was locked shut. The adults also tried, to no avail. By then we were all terrified. The room had become so cold we could see our breath condensing in the air.

Eventually, I began to ask for help by praying to Jesus. Because of my Grandma's religious sharing with me, he meant the most to me. I knew he represented love and I felt it in my heart. I knew I could call upon him for help at any time and it would be given. I remembered the quote, "Ask and ye shall receive" and so I asked. Almost immediately the cold disappeared, the light fixture slowed to a stop and we all made a mad rush for the door. When the door was open, there was my Mum. She'd come out to search for me and was met by five people in a terrified state. She was really angry with me and I was dragged home and given a good hiding.

The next day I was hauled along to sit in front of Father Healey, our parish priest. Mum made me tell him all that had happened and he offered to visit the house and have a look.

On entering, he asked to visit the bedroom directly

above the room we'd been in. On returning, he told us he felt it necessary to bless the room and told the owners that the house was now clear. I never went back to the house again, but I learned about the power of prayer that night.

SCHOOL, BOYS AND BEYOND

"The heart that loves is forever young."
– Greek proverb

I attended Saint Anne's Catholic school in Heaton
Chapel at the other end of town, a two-hour round trip.
I dreaded the daily trip as I was the only school kid
wearing a Catholic uniform. The other kids from
Brinnington all went to the local state school. I stood
out like a sore thumb. They would regularly be waiting
for me at the bus stop and it wasn't to make friends.

When I mustered the courage to go in to the school,
I loved the art and music classes. It was as if there was a
switch in my head that turned itself off during the other
subjects, especially religion. I just didn't get it, although
one boy in my class named Mark obviously did – he's
now the Bishop of Shrewsbury. I had my stars and my
'imaginary' friends – all the guidance I needed.

I was always in trouble for not paying attention to
the lesson and wandering off into the skies in my head.
Needless to say, that didn't go down too well with the
teachers and fairly often a good whacking on the hand

with the cane would shake me back to earth. The nuns were the worst. They seemed to take real pleasure in the process. They never smiled and I often thought that maybe if they took off those dark-colored habits they wore they would feel much more comfortable and maybe cheer up a little. How were we supposed to absorb the lessons of Catholicism if the people teaching it were as miserable as hell? They should have brought in my Grandma to teach. She knew what she was talking about.

I could hardly wait for the day to end when I could rejoin my best friend Yvonne and take the bus to the town's youth clubs where we would dance our worries away.

Yvonne joined our school late on. We were 13 years old when she and I became glued together. Yvonne's Mum ran the King's Head in Stockport, an historic pub, haunted by old souls, probably still longing for a drink. It never scared us though, and we loved to help out there, emptying the coins from the pool tables and washing the glasses in exchange for crisps, fizzy drinks (called 'pop' where I came from) and most important, the money to go dancing. I spent every minute I could with her.

We were kindred spirits with much in common. Her Mum and stepfather drank quite heavily too. I regularly bore witness to Yvonne being hit by her Mum for misbehaving. She was there one day when it was my turn to be abused. Jerry blew out of control and grabbed me by the neck and with full force smashed my head against a wall in the hallway. My head had a huge bump on it for quite a while afterward and to this day I can't remember what initiated the attack. We just learned to stay out of his way as much as possible, wandering around the streets for want of anything better to do.

On two occasions, I almost came to a sticky end. The first time was during a very hot summer afternoon. I was making my regular journey back to Brinnington across the vale from my Auntie Teresa's house in Reddish when I noticed a man watching me as I began the climb up the steep hill ahead. He shouted for me to stop but my intuition told me that he meant me harm. I climbed, desperately trying to outrun him, but he got close enough to grab my ankle. I almost gave up but managed to shake him off, terrified and crying. Using all the strength I could muster, I made it to the top of the hill and carried on running to the nearest house, which happened to be my Uncle Bob's. I didn't dare look behind, knowing I would collapse with fear if the stranger was still pursuing me. I finally reached the house and ran in the open door, eventually looking out to see the man, who had been right on my heels, lurking outside.

My cousin Jane and I watched from the window as he hung around for several minutes before finally retreating. I was shocked by the ordeal but it never occurred to us to ring the police for fear of getting into trouble with our parents. Much later, I ventured back outside and headed home, only to find an empty house.

The second close call happened when I spent the

night at Yvonne's pub in Portwood one night. It was quite late in the evening and Yvonne's Mum was angry with her for not cleaning the kitchen that day. To avoid further confrontation and another good hiding, we offered to walk to the chip shop to pick up a takeaway supper. Off we went, talking all the way about how we would one day escape all this violence and run off together to a wonderful far-off place.

All of a sudden, a car screeched to a halt on the road beside us, a door flung open and we saw three men inside. One of them jumped out and tried to grab me and pull me into the car. I screamed and Yvonne tried to pull me away from him. It was a real struggle to break free as he gripped my wrist but I succeeded and we made a run for it, only to see the car speeding alongside. We made it into the chip shop in tears and begged the Chinese lady behind the counter to phone for the police. She told us there was no need and we were to stay in the shop until the car drove off. Eventually the men gave up on and the car sped away.

We got up our courage and ran for our lives back to Yvonne's. Instead of sympathy on arrival, we were severely reprimanded for causing yet more problems. I knew in my heart that my invisible protectors were looking after me on both these occasions and during many other painful experiences.

I felt that I was being shown many aspects of life and that they were somehow preparing me to help others in the future. I rarely shared my spiritual feelings with my friend as it wasn't the sort of thing people spoke about freely at that time and we were far too occupied with our teenage pursuits of trying to keep up with the fashions of the day and finding boyfriends – though my experiences in that department weren't exactly what you'd call normal.

At thirteen, I was walking to the local shops with my boyfriend when another boy started an argument with him. The lad pulled out a knife and stabbed my boyfriend in the chest. He was rushed to hospital where the doctors discovered that the knife had penetrated and collapsed one of his lungs.

I was stunned to witness such a thing at such close proximity yet this was common behaviour in our neighborhood where many boys were involved in drugs and crime as a means of coping with the environment. A short time later another boy and great friend of mine was found dead in his garden from a lethal dose of heroin. Life was day-to-day survival for many who lived in the housing estates.

More sadness came four years later. While working as a children's shoe fitter in Stockport town center I dated a local policeman. He was very shy and gentle and not at all the usual sort of 'bobby' to be found on the police force in our area. He told me his parents couldn't accept his choice of career and had refused any contact until he came to his senses. They'd had high hopes of his becoming an airline pilot but Allen wanted to follow his heart's promptings. On our usual day to meet he didn't turn up at my workplace. I became really worried about him, knowing his fragile state of mind. I had no way of contacting him as he lived out in the countryside and all I could think of was check the local newspaper.

I almost passed out with shock when I read that he had been found at a nearby park, having pointed and fired a sawed-off shotgun at his head. He had died instantly at only 21 years old. I was totally devastated and had to take weeks off work to recover. I agonised that I could have somehow prevented this tragedy. In hindsight, I can see that this event propelled me further into my search for a way to both help and understand my fellow man.

After living in Stockport for only a year, Yvonne and her Mum moved away to manage a pub in Wrexham, Wales. I was right behind her and school went by the wayside. I simply could not have gone on living there without my best friend. I loved the train ride down, having no fear whatsoever of traveling as it was getting me as far away as possible from my own dysfunctional home life. The freedom was pure heaven. Yvonne's Mum Rose met me and hid me in the back room of the pub just before Yvonne was home from school. She told Yvonne that she had a little surprise for her and I jumped out, laughing. The excitement of seeing each other again was almost unbearable. We immediately started to plan the adventures we would have together during the six-week summer holidays.

I left school at the age of fifteen without any qualifications that didn't bother me in the least. It felt more natural to me to find my own way and see what life had to offer. I worked just about everywhere after that. I had, in fact, started to work at an early age. I was ten years old when I worked on the local pop delivery van, and, at thirteen I worked weekends, Saturdays on the market selling gloves and Sundays in the town centre chip shop. It meant I could hold my head up as there was no money to be had at home.

I got a job in a small supermarket in Heaton Moor that only lasted a few weeks. During that time, a tall young boy from my old school came in. He seemed to appear out of nowhere and spoke to me briefly. I was unaware that he was one of a group of boys that had been following me around with schoolboy crushes. It was all very flattering but he seemed far too young for me to take any real notice. However, 33 years later I was to have another, much more surprising, encounter with him.

Settling Down

"Some pursue happiness, others create it."
   – Unknown

My first full-time job was as a machinist making Levi jeans at an old industrial mill in Portwood, Stockport. The money was excellent but the job was boring, so I found a position as a trainee in a very posh hair salon in the centre of town. I loved it there and found I had a natural ability to style hair – until one day, instead of brushing hair, the manageress preferred that l brush the outside yard. I really began to question whether or not she liked me when I had to brush the yard even though it was December and there was thick snow on the ground. So I took it as a hint that it was time to move on again.

   I checked the jobs page in the Manchester Evening News – a fruitful pursuit in those days of abundant jobs. I found that our local butcher, Titterton's, was looking for a shop assistant to work in its factory outlet, a five-minute walk from home. I decided to go for it and use the job as a steppingstone to something better. I was simply going with the flow and had much more on my mind, like dating the three boyfriends I had attracted. I was never short of attention from the opposite sex. I really loved that job, and it was there that I met Les, who was to become my loving husband and caring father of our two wonderful children.

We first met while walking home after work. I knew he liked me because he would come into the shop more often than necessary. Next door to the shop was the factory where he worked as a butcher. It was raining that afternoon and I looked over my shoulder to see that he was walking behind me, getting wet. I asked him if he wanted to walk under my umbrella and we talked all the way back to our homes, a few streets apart.

We hit it off straight away and started meeting at his house on Thursday evenings when his parents were out. After we watched Top of the Pops together he would walk me back home. We soon ventured farther afield when we discovered Rumours, a new nightclub in Portwood that played our favorite soul and funk. We shared a love of music and the concepts and messages the songs awoke in our minds. Marvin Gaye, Stevie Wonder, and Earth Wind & Fire were among the many great artists we listened to.

At that time, it was a big thing to date someone of color. Les's grandfather was well known as one of the first Jamaicans to arrive in the UK. My Mum and her family remembered him as 'old Mr Wint' when they were growing up. Mum said they were scared of him at first as he was so dark-skinned and nobody had ever seen anyone like him before.

People would walk past his house in Cheadle Heath just to have a look at him, and would always find him cheerful with a huge smile on his face. As for Les, at the time of our meeting Michael Jackson was the pop idol of the day and having an afro meant instant attention from onlookers. Les's was totally natural but his friend Brian had to go to the hairdressers for a perm, an occasion which always brought a joke or two from Les.

I was so proud to walk out with him in his bell-bottom trousers and tight-fitting shirts with big pointy collars. I never gave it a second thought that he was Jamaican until one night when a group of rowdy young men started shouting at us. I hadn't a clue whose name it was they were chanting until I asked my Mum later that night. It was Enoch Powell, the Conservative Party politician who was said to be a racist.

My love for Les was all that mattered to me so this incident only made me love him more. We hardly left each other's side and would stay at each other's houses. We longed for our own place but with little funds coming in from our jobs it was impossible. However, we were able to save for the holiday of our life and were one of the first couples to book a flight to Florida on Freddie Laker's new airline. We spent two glorious weeks there, one on Miami Beach and the other in the Florida Keys.

After a couple of years of dating, out of the blue I became pregnant with our first child. We were surprised but delighted and immediately made plans to marry. We did this on Friday the 13th, November 1981, at our local registry office, much to the dismay of our families who thought it an unlucky date for a marriage. We didn't pay any attention to superstition and our happy marriage lasted eighteen years. Our son Ashley, the first light of our life, came into the world six months later. Our second child, Stacey, was born six years later.

We applied to the local housing office for a place to live and they offered us a one-bedroom apartment close to the town center. We gratefully accepted and moved in when I was four months pregnant. All went well until I began feeling ill and was taken to the hospital for tests. They discovered I had toxemia, a serious condition of elevated blood pressure resulting in too much protein in my blood. Left untreated, it might have led to deadly consequences. I later learned that it was one of the leading causes of maternal and infant mortality worldwide.

At the time, I had very little knowledge of nutrition. I thought I had carte blanche to eat whatever I wanted, as I was now eating for two. Les would bring me porridge before he left for work at 6 am and I would be hungry again by 9 am and eat several rounds of thickly buttered toast. Then after lunch came afternoon tea, biscuits and packets of crisps. If that was not enough, there would be a big evening meal followed by a late supper.

When it came time to give birth, ten days overdue, I weighed in at a whopping 190 pounds, which was far too heavy for my 5'3" frame and my initial weigh-in of 130 lbs. It was a horrible delivery. It took fifteen hours of full-on induced labor and the pain medication had no effect on me whatsoever. My baby was stuck and the only other doctor on duty that night was already attending another difficult delivery. I was sliced open, forceps were employed, and they pulled so hard I was almost dragged right off the table. We survived the ordeal and my beautiful baby boy entered this world somewhat reluctantly on May 12th, 1982.

Finding Healing

"All healing starts in the mind."
– Alison Stormwolf

I was trying to make sense of why I felt like jumping from my three-story window instead of being the serene and capable mother I read about in all the baby manuals and saw on television. What was wrong with me? My life never seemed to go smoothly.

In the weeks following my traumatic delivery I received little care from the health professionals. I had a real need for some answers. It was a constant struggle to make ends meet and cope with my ongoing depression. I adored my son. He had become my life and reason for living. I had to get well so I made an appointment at the general surgery. Surely they would have some idea why I was feeling this way.

My doctor's solution was to put me on Prozac, the anti-depressant 'wonder drug' that wasn't so wonder-full for me. My depression continued.

I began to question the Western medical model and went in search of self-help books. I read many that were useful but offered no real relief until one day, at our local Tuesday market, my eye was drawn to a book, The Third Eye by an oddly-named author, Lobsang Rampa. I handed over a pound and took it home.

After putting my son to bed that night, I sat down to begin the book.

I couldn't put it down. I was fascinated by the story of a Tibetan monk who had been raised in one of his country's monasteries. I had the strange notion that I had been there. After I had finished the book, I immediately wanted to read the second volume in the series. It was so mind-expanding and affirming to read about some of the mysteries I had often thought about since my early childhood, including seeing and hearing beings from other realms.

Around this time, my Grandma started to become confused and would wander off into the street in her nightclothes. It was awful to witness my all-knowing Grandma becoming so forgetful and frightened. Mum brought Grandma to live with her but the dementia worsened and she couldn't cope while having my sisters and brother still living at home in such a small place. Mum had to make the agonizing decision to place her in a home for the elderly. Bless her soul, she didn't survive for long deciding to make her exit while her children had taken a day trip to Blackpool. My own grieving was minimal, as I knew I would still be able to talk with her. To me, nobody really died. They just went on with their bodiless journey.

One day while shopping, I came across a new type of store I hadn't seen before. The sign outside said 'Isis' and I felt drawn to enter, thinking perhaps they would have books inside. I was immediately struck by the wonderful smell of incense and the serene music that was playing. I could have remained there forever. I felt such a remembrance of this stuff – the candles, stained glasswork and oh, the crystals!

As I turned around, in a sort of hypnotic trance, I looked into the eyes of the girl behind the sales desk and felt myself shiver. I instantly recognized her, but how could I? We had never met. She smiled and asked if there was anything she could help me with. I mentioned I was looking for a volume by Lobsang Rampa and couldn't quite believe it when she replied that she had the collection herself. Another affirmation of 'Ask and you shall receive'!

Her name was Sue and we spent hours together, sharing our interest in the esoteric content of the book. It seemed obvious that we had some deep connection with Tibet. She told me she had studied Reiki – a healing method that could be passed on to others, and that she was a Reiki master teacher.

I was totally in my element and experiencing deja vu. I explained to Sue that most of my life I had felt out of sync with my Catholic upbringing, that I honored its principles, but felt constrained by it. I also shared that I needed some help with my ongoing depression. Sue offered to give me a Reiki healing session and I accepted. I could hardly wait until the next day for my appointment.

The next morning I arrived and was led upstairs to a peaceful room with a massage bed. Sue asked me to lie down and used her hands to channel the healing energy into my body. She started at my head and I instantly felt at peace for the first time in years. I don't remember drifting off into a deep state of relaxation. I do remember recalling the wonderful colors I had seen in my mind's eye after the session was over. Those significant colors again! I felt so good after the session that I knew I had to learn how to do this for others.

After the session, while I drank the water Sue offered, she shared her belief that all people have natural healing abilities and that it would be a pleasure to initiate me. She told me there were three degrees of training in Reiki, undertaken in stages. I would take the first degree, then it was recommended to wait about three months before taking the second.

After that initial session my depression vanished! I made the decision to dedicate my life to helping others who might be in need of Reiki's healing force. Sue and I became inseparable over the next three months and I completed all the training during that time. My next chapter of becoming a healing channel had begun. I ultimately read and digested the remaining Lobsang Rampa volumes.

Things were never quite the same after that. They say that when we make a change within ourselves, the world around us changes. That was certainly the case with me. Over the next few years, I practiced healing and working with the images in my mind I'd had since childhood but which now became focused and meaningful.

They became ever more colorful and vivid and I began to trust the ever-present guidance from what I'd come to call the Star Beings. I was now witnessing many healing transformations and came to understand that there are many dimensions to our lives.

FROM WASHINGTON, D.C. TO CORNWALL

"As human beings our greatness lies not so much in being able to remake the world ... as in being able to remake ourselves."
– Mahatma Gandhi

During this time Les, Ashley and I went to live in Washington, D.C. for a year. We lived in McLean, a suburban area of Virginia, where most residents were foreign diplomats. Ashley attended the local kindergarten and I'll always remember dropping him off that first morning and picking him up again later. The change in him was startling. He came running across the school yard full of enthusiasm, telling me how, first thing, all the kids had stood on their desks while the teacher told them how special and unique they all were and that they could be anything they wanted to be. He couldn't wait to return the next day. I thought of my own first day at Saint Joseph's and how the last thing I wanted was to go back. Why hadn't our teachers been so positive and empowered us to express our unique gifts?

40

Les got a job with a local flooring company, eventually installing the floor coverings for both the Pentagon and Dulles Airport. Because we needed more money to live on, I put my healing work on the back burner and found a job selling mink coats. Winters were quite severe in Washington and many women owned not one, but several furs. Having so little our selves, I was always overwhelmed when a customer came in to purchase a coat for $20,000 or more. It was 1984 and that kind of money could buy a home back in the UK.

We were living and working in the US illegally. My boss at the time was also illegally employed having arrived from Argentina to seek a better life. One day, I took Ashley for ice cream at Baskin Robbins. I got into a conversation with a local man who was looking for someone to help him demonstrate his new body composition machines. I quickly offered my services because taking the job meant I could look after Ashley during the week, leaving Les to mind him on the weekend. I enjoyed working in the George Washington Memorial Center and my daily pay equaled my entire week's salary selling fur coats.

One of the girls we shared the house with in McLean was dating one of the Washington Redskin football players so we were invited to lots of pool parties and trips to the beach. All in all, it was a very exciting and wonderful time but my longing for family and friends brought about our return after a year. The time spent there and the people I met affected me profoundly. I felt more at home there than in the UK. I also knew that one day I would return, perhaps for good.

We had been back for some time when we decided to try for another baby and in no time I was pregnant with my beautiful daughter Stacey. To say that the birth was different than Ashley's would be a complete understatement. This time I ate lots of raw food and instead of the 60 lbs I gained while expecting my son, I only gained 16. I felt great throughout my pregnancy and all went beautifully with my baby girl weighing in at a healthy 7 lbs 3 oz. I attribute Stacey's easy arrival to my healthy lifestyle of meditation, healing work and high-quality food.

The business of homemaking and work continued and I was very happy with life although I began to have that familiar urge to discover more. We decided to buy a touring caravan so that we could afford more holiday time with the children. We would take two holidays a year to Anglesey and Cornwall, two places steeped in ancient history that fascinated me. We found a fabulous campsite in the village of Perranporth, not far from Newquay, where we could walk down to the beach from our cliff-top site. The children loved the place as much as we did. The area was famous for water sports. We fitted them with wetsuits and surfboards and they took full advantage of the camp's busy entertainment program. Their favorite activity was the evening disco and to this day music and socializing play a big part in their lives.

I felt I had past life connections here. I would take the family to the stone circles that littered the area, and

on one occasion we drove onto Bodmin Moor to visit
The Hurlers, a well-known monument. It contained
three circles consisting of between 25 and 30 stones
each as well as two standing stones, the Pipers. Legend
says the stones are men punished by St Cleer for playing
football on the Lord's day and that they are
uncountable.

On these excursions, we would take our cine-camera
to record our visits. This time, our trusty camera refused
to work when we were anywhere near the stones. As
soon as we walked away, it would switch itself on. It was
as though the stones were not anxious to be
photographed and made sure they wouldn't be. It
delighted the children that these kinds of things
happened.

We were also drawn to the world-famous Witchcraft
Museum originally built on the Isle of Man in 1951 by
Cecil Williamson and later moved to the picturesque
village of Boscastle. Williamson's interest in witchcraft
and magic began as a child in North Bovey, Devon when
he befriended the local witch, an elderly woman who
was being attacked by locals claiming she bewitched
cattle.

While working on a tobacco plantation in Rhodesia,
Williamson investigated the craft of African witch
doctors. He developed his interest on returning to
Britain in the 1930s, mixing with leading experts of the
day including Margaret Murray, Montague Summers
and Aleister Crowley, later becoming close friends with
the influential Wiccan, Gerald Gardner. He also worked

as an agent for MI6, collating the occult interests of the Nazis. He was fascinated by the old ways of rural village witchcraft and became a practitioner himself. Today the museum stands against all odds, having relocated to Boscastle in 1960 and surviving the worst floods in British history on August 16th, 2004.

On another camping trip to Cornwall, just before dawn, the children and Les were asleep when I saw a uniformed man walk into the caravan. He was wearing a red soldier's uniform and carried a lantern. He smiled at me and walked on straight through the back of the van, disappearing into the night. The next day I enquired at the desk and learned that he walked the camp most nights and was seen by those who were sensitive. Cornwall is steeped in magic and mystery and I felt it was important that the children had access to this sort of information. I wanted them to know that there was much more to life than what most called 'reality'.

LESSONS

"Be humble for you are made of earth. Be noble for you are made of stars."
– Serbian proverb

Most of my friends during that time would visit my house to take part in meditation sessions. I didn't raise my children with any kind of religious practice as I had been. I wanted to give them the freedom to find their own way. I always trusted in a soul beyond the physical realm and understood that it knew all. They were made aware of the need to treat others with love and respect above all. For a while, they both attended the little Christian Sunday School at the end of our street. Other than that, any religious information they received came from their school.

Early on in my awakening to the energies that worked with me, I had two very distinct, hard lessons to learn regarding the issue of healing permission. I believe that all healing is simply giving love although from these two lessons I learned to only use my healing gift when asked.

The first lesson happened while my son, age nine, lay with his head on my lap watching TV. He said, "Mum, please don't do any healing while I'm lying here. I just want to sleep". After a few minutes I felt the energy start to flow through me into him and thought it would do no harm. Within moments he jumped off my knee, looking startled, and said, "Mum, I asked you not to do that. I left my body and was up on the ceiling looking down at us. Please, Mum I don't want you to do that again!" Episode over and done with and off he went to have his bath before bed. It made me more aware of the power of my energy to impact others.

The second lesson happened years later. I was overtaken by my need to help my mother with her pain. I visited during one of her very low points and we talked for hours while she told me about her difficult childhood and how the memories had stayed with her. She had always felt she hadn't been a good parent. I let her know, "Mum, we all chose to be with each other in this lifetime. You were the best Mum we could have asked for. Please come to peace with this". She began to cry and I walked over to sit with her and put my arms around her. Again, I felt the energy begin to flow and I didn't stop it, as to me it was just all the love I could muster up to give her.

As I was traveling home my cousin called. She said Mum had 'gone ballistic' drinking and throwing things about her home. Mum's unconscious memories had come through too suddenly and she was unable to cope with them. I rushed back to talk things through and she told me she had felt so much love that it was unbearable for her. She knew, she said, that she had created everything in her life and just had to get on with what she had come to learn.

Changes

"Life belongs to the living and he who lives must be prepared for change."
– Johann Wolfgang von Goethe

I wanted to learn how to use words mindfully while helping others. I thought that I was missing something in the silence of the healing sessions. I found that my local college offered an evening psychology course and Les was more than happy to arrange his work shift so I could enroll. I loved every minute of the program and after gaining my qualification was left with a thirst for more.

As I began to grow in confidence, I was disturbed to find that my husband felt that our interests had diverged and we were growing apart. Admittedly, I'd lost interest in going to the local pub with him, and we found it difficult to share a conversation in the way we used to. What could I do? I'd changed from the young girl he'd met at eighteen. I so wanted us to remain together, not only for the sake of the children, but also for us. We had so many wonderful memories together.

48

Les had been my life and my first love. I was devastated when it ended, following a series of events that precipitated the parting.

In December 2000, I came across an advert for a talk on past lives, a subject that had always intrigued me. Was there really such a thing as reincarnation? The advert, displayed in a local post office window, seemed to have a power that drew me in. I felt the same tingling sensation that usually occurred when I had to move toward something so I immediately picked up the phone and booked a seat.

Several nights later I was on my way to the event. As I entered the room, I joined five others eagerly awaiting the speaker. He walked in confidently and took a seat at the front of the small group. Oddly, as he began to talk, I felt myself becoming drowsy and struggled to keep my eyes open. Nevertheless I was fascinated and hung onto every word of his two-hour presentation.

The speaker's name was John. I approached him after the talk and he told me about his work as a hypnotherapist. Realising that this approach could bring positive change to any circumstance, and could complement my healing practice, I asked him where he'd trained.

That first meeting brought about the ending to my whole reason for living at that time and I will remember it for the rest of my life. I wouldn't have attended that night if I'd had any inkling of what lay ahead, and what I would endure in the name of self-development. This was the most challenging time of my life and lasted for ten

long years. Did I create this situation for my awakening
in this lifetime or did life have a plan for me all along?
All I can say is that I had no choice in the matter of
leaving my husband, children, two dogs and family
home.

My Mum said John was a Svengali. My sisters said I
had changed overnight since attending that talk. All I
knew was that that I had to learn more from this man.
My husband had enough of my seemingly endless
searching and the amount of time I was spending
around John. We were fighting almost constantly about
my relationship with him and it caused Les to feel
hugely insecure. If the shoe had been on the other foot, I
would have felt exactly the same way.

There would be no reconciliation between us and we
agreed that I would be the one to leave. I was
heartbroken. I asked the children if they would come
with me, but how could they? I couldn't provide for
them. I had no money of my own. Every penny went to
the family's upkeep. I remember that night lay on the
bed with my thirteen-year-old daughter, trying to help
her understand why I had to leave. How could I possibly
expect her to understand? I felt as though my heart was
being ripped out of my chest. I knew what she was going
through. She put on a brave face and said, "Mum, just
go. Find your peace, because you haven't been happy for
a long time". We both lay there for what seemed an
eternity, trying to pretend this wasn't happening.

As the days went on I experienced sheer agony
during the process of leaving my beautiful family and

little dogs. I didn't give a thought to the house or any of the material things we had worked so hard to acquire. I wanted them to have everything. I needed nothing. I only wanted to keep us all together somehow. I stupidly hoped that I was simply going through some mid-life crisis and that I would be returning as soon as this nightmare ended. That was not to be. As I expected, the children stuck by their father and the life they had always known. I would have had it no other way.

Magical Anglesey

"You can't cross the sea merely by standing and staring at the water."
– Rabindranath Tagore

I initially rented a small house on the Isle of Anglesey, a place Les and I had visited each year of our marriage. I walked the cliffs daily, crying endlessly. When would my pain go away? I needed to be alone while I attempted to come to terms with my life.

John came to visit a couple of times a week. Again my inner voice was guiding me. There was something I had requested for this life and I had to carry on one day at a time. I was certain all would be revealed in time.

One day I decided to take a trip across the island to Holyhead. I had to move on and try to start mixing with other people again. The little money I had was running out fast, so I had no option but to go to the local employment centre for help. I tried to hold it together but ended up breaking down in front of the clerk handling my case. It was obvious that I was mentally unfit for work so they referred me to the local doctor.

After my assessment, I was told that I was in danger of having a nervous breakdown and was once again given anti-depressants and just enough money to scrape by on.

Soon after, John came to visit me again. On our walk around Holyhead we discovered The Harvest Moon Cafe. We went in to order coffee and there, standing behind the counter, was Judy, a beautiful shining soul. She and her sister had purchased the quirky little building a few years before. They were vegans and naturally made it a vegan cafe with a difference – a healing-cum-drop-in-centre. The food was delicious and healing love was in every molecule of the place. Judy welcomed us with open arms as she did every person who walked through her doors.

She told me that drifters would often walk in off the ferry that was only a stone's throw away. The boats would leave several times a day for the port in Dublin and there were times when she had taken people home with her to give them a meal or a bed. I instantly felt completely at ease with her. I shared my story and within no time she offered me a place to stay in return for working in the cafe. I was grateful I had found a place where I could also be of help.

I stayed with Judy for a few months, helping out, making and serving food, and doing what I could when folks came in wanting a shoulder to lean on. One of the many friends I made in my time living on that magical mother isle was Gwen, a unique loving woman who had opened a small spiritual gift shop across the road from the Harvest Moon. She was there most days simply radiating her love to all who entered her space as she does to this day, though she is no longer to be found in the shop. Many times I would pop in to sit with her and sometimes stand in to give her a break. The people of the island knew that they could turn to her in times of need and she would always find time for them.

One day the door of the cafe opened and in walked Roger and Dorothy, who were to become a large part of my life. They lived in the middle of the island in Llanrhyddlad, on fifteen beautiful acres of land with a lake around which they had planted 13,000 trees to replenish the island's stock. They called their land Orsedd Isaf, which translates as 'Lower Throne'. It's said that Druids once occupied much of Anglesey and many visitors say they feel their energy.

Roger and Dorothy had heard through the grapevine on the very small island that I was in need of a permanent place to stay. They had taken the trip into town to offer me their little cottage next to the big house where they lived. I was so grateful for their kindness and offered to help them in any way I could. They housed and cared for twenty-two cats and six dogs and took in waifs and strays from all over the island. I guess I was one of them.

About this time, John came to live with me. The land here provided a very clear and receptive environment. I spent every possible moment gazing at my stars. There was minimal light pollution in the centre of the island and for once I had the precious time

I needed to explore my inner world. I would go into deep trance states and it became easy to channel loving entities. I learned to let go of my personality and travel deeper and deeper into myself. I went looking for love and found it, discovering I was part of a greater whole.

I also had experiences of my many past lives, reliving strong memories of a lady of high society, a train driver, a boy chimney sweep, the latter illuminating my present-day claustrophobia and all giving me greater understanding of my current existence, although the pain of my children's absence never seemed to fully ease. It became normal for me to tap into the Oneness, the vast library of information that is available to all of us, the source of everything, the mind of God.

Friendship With a Druid

"God writes the gospel not in the Bible alone, but also on trees, and in the flowers and clouds and stars."
– Martin Luther

One of the most enigmatic people I ever met while living on Angelsey is Kristoffer Hughes, a practising Druid. We met one day while I was working in Holyhead. As soon as we began to talk it was evident we had much in common.

Kris and I share the same Scorpio birth sign. He says we're both as mad as hatters and we both have a huge fascination with physical death, although Kris knows a lot more about that subject as he spends his days with the deceased. He has been a pathologist's assistant for the last 15 years or more and is probably the only one in the world who plays the harp during his working day.

It was his height that first caught my attention standing as he does at 6'5" tall and looking strikingly handsome in his Druid regalia. Kris was born on Anglesey and chose the priesthood after leaving school.

After a short time in Bible School, he began to doubt the scriptures he was studying. He voiced his opinions, found they didn't go down very well with his teachers and that was that. Eschewing organised religion, Kris pursued his love of nature and Awen, the Welsh word for divine inspiration of the bards. We spent a great deal of time together sharing our views on life, both arriving at the conclusion that All is One and One is All.

We laughed almost constantly whenever we were together, usually at the insanity of being here on planet Earth. Kris was adept at reading the Tarot using the Kabbalistic method and would regularly give talks at Orsedd Isaf on the Celtic traditions. One of our best times together was at a Druid camp in Monmouth, not far from the forest of Dean. This was my first time at an event like this and Kris was full of mischievous delight at what was to come, as I was well known for my need to be clean and tidy. No one informed me that the lavatory was in the middle of a field in the form of a wooden box with a ten-foot drop filled with straw. I just couldn't get up the courage to go resulting in us having to drive into Monmouth where there was a public toilet. As if that wasn't a total nuisance, we also had to shower in a horse stall powered by a wood-burning stove. At times, we could hardly stand from laughing so hard.

Evenings were spent storytelling and drinking mead while sitting around our campfire. Kris presented a fascinating talk on death. The camp was an amazing experience, ending five days later with a grand finale. We formed a huge circle of 300 friends, all Druids apart from me. I stood still, wondering what was coming next as I could see Kris and his partner on the opposite side of the circle pointing toward me and laughing.

Then I saw it! A huge horn filled with mead from which we all had to sip to toast the end of the gathering. They knew that another of my idiosyncrasies was a fear of sharing drinking vessels. At least a hundred people had drunk from the horn by the time it got to me and I was hot and sweaty with the thought of having to put it to my mouth. As it was passed to me, I turned the enormous thing round to drink out of the other side, in full sight of the assembled gathering. I thought the lads were going to collapse they were laughing so much. From that day on I was called Germolena Lil, a name they still call me from time to time although I have since conquered the phobia.

We had such a fantastic time that we didn't want to return to Anglesey and drove down to Boscastle in Cornwall for a few days before returning to Monmouth for another camp, this time for the healing arts. We'd just had a very large breakfast at one of the village cafes, when Kris jumped up to announce he was seriously in need of the toilet only to find there wasn't one on the premises. The owner pointed him in the direction of a public convenience at the other end of the street. Kris bolted off like a racehorse creating much laughter once again.

After twenty minutes, I began to get worried about him. When he arrived back at the car he was quick to explain. "Bloody hell, I bumped straight into that Spice woman, you know, Sporty Spice. Well, I ran over to her and said, 'Hello my name's Kristoffer and I'm a Druid. It's very nice to meet you but I'm in the middle of a medical emergency. I've got diarrhea!' She won't forget me in a hurry!" More laughter as we made our return to the camp.

Two weeks later we returned to Anglesey, thoroughly elated from our adventures and still laughing at my expense. We still manage to get together occasionally as Kris is now a busy well-known author of several books on Druidry and the Celtic tradition.

TRIALS IN THAILAND

"This too will pass."
– Proverb

After six months John and I both missed our family so much that we decided it was time to return to Stockport for a while. Not a day went by that I didn't long to be with my children and family again. I thought the crying would never end. I just couldn't come to terms with it. Why all this suffering?

We returned and stayed at John's mother's house until we could find a place to live. I was able to see the children briefly and spent a little time with my Mum who by now was virtually housebound with crippling rheumatoid arthritis. We talked for hours and she was concerned about where I would end up. I didn't know myself, only that I had to live one day at a time.

John's mother was also unwell. She had emphysema, a progressive and debilitating lung disease and it was very difficult for her with us around. Tension was high so we decided to travel as far away as possible in the hope that in the peace and quiet we would discover what to do next.

The cost of living in Thailand seemed affordable to us, and a week later we were on a plane to Bangkok. It was everything I'd heard about: fast, noisy and heavily polluted air. By the time we arrived at Khao San Road – the meeting area for all newly arrived backpackers, I was beginning to wonder how I was going to cope with the pollution. From a young age I'd slept with the window open needing fresh air and unfortunately in Bangkok there wasn't any. It was incredibly humid and after walking for a few minutes, I felt exhausted. We checked into a hotel intending to leave Bangkok as quickly as possible. I couldn't believe that many visitors could last here for very long.

The next day we took a coach to Koh Samui, a beautiful island off the east coast, and moved into a hotel room on the beach. At last I could breathe again! It was the sort of place you'd see on the front cover of a travel brochure, an absolute paradise for the sun seeker, though I still found the humidity very uncomfortable.

On one memorable night I wandered out onto the beach and lay beneath my stars. The temperature was still quite high but much more comfortable than during the day and I lay back in the silence with tears in my eyes wishing I was back home with my children. I thought that I was losing my mind and prayed for clarity. As I stared at the sky I counted seven shooting stars shooting across the cobalt sky. I took this as a message from the universe that all would be well in time.

I began to question John's behavior. He would go off alone for hours leaving me frantic with worry only to return to the room to find him in bed. When I asked if he was OK, he would completely ignore me until I cried with frustration. These occasions could last several days without John speaking a word. When he finally spoke to me he acted as if nothing had happened. I felt a long way from home and began to count the days till my return to the UK.

As we traveled from town to town I observed many large and ornate golden temples and so many people living hand to mouth. I saw the monks walking the streets wearing their orange robes carrying begging bowls, collecting money for their temples. It was that same old feeling I'd had about my own early religious conditioning and I didn't get this religion either. So much wealth wrapped up in these extravagant buildings when so many people were starving. My heart ached for people to wake up and share what they had with each other.

I found it hard to cope with the animal cruelty I witnessed on a daily basis. One day while we were traveling in the back of an open-topped taxi the driver ran over one of the many stray dogs that lived on the streets. We looked back to see the animal lying in the road writhing in agony. The driver didn't stop the vehicle or even bat an eyelid. Apparently dogs were considered vermin and were fair game for anyone with a gun. It was the straw that broke the camels back for me. It was time to leave Thailand.

Even though the view of the stars was the clearest I'd ever seen in my entire life, I simply couldn't come to terms with what was going on around me. After a week of living with John's moods, I decided to return early. The local people didn't speak a word of English and I thought I was going to lose my mind from having no one to talk with. John watched me leave in a taxi and I headed out to the airport. He waved me off, saying that he was enjoying himself far too much to leave and had decided to go on to Singapore. I cried the whole way home.

Moving On

"We are the cosmos made conscious and life is the means by which the universe understands itself."
– Brian Cox

I stayed with my Mum for the next week, and we talked about my pressing problem of finding a place to live. Mum of course, said I was welcome to stay with her as long as I needed. Like me, my family was very concerned that John could let me travel all that way home alone but for some reason I still went to meet him at Manchester Airport on his return. I wanted some answers, to find out why he had been so strange in Thailand. He arrived back looking relaxed and on the way to Stockport begged me to understand, promising he'd worked things out and things would be good between us from now on.

I had to give it another try. I found a place to live in Marple, close to where the children lived, and managed to put down the deposit required for a six-month lease. We moved in that week and John's depressive episodes became fewer and less extreme. I thought perhaps over time I might be able to help him heal.

After settling into our new place, I felt the urge to do more training and sought out online courses. It felt like the right time to pursue a qualification in Hypnotherapy and my search led me to the Atkinson-Ball College of Hypnotherapy and Hypno-Healing. A ten-weekend course was about to begin in Liverpool City center. Perfect! Hypnosis was something I had always been interested in and would provide me with an extra skill set to add to my healing practice. The course turned out to be one of the best I had ever taken.

After I gained my qualification I found myself yearning to go back to the magical isle of Anglesey. I was dearly missing my new friends there. I made a few telephone calls to check on rentals and was offered an affordable cottage on South Stack Road not far from Holyhead Mountain. I jumped at the offer and John made the decision to come too although this time he was reluctant to leave his sons behind. I was comfortable with being able to return when I wanted to see my family and have them come to stay with me at the cottage occasionally.

I could once again walk the beautiful cliffs and beaches in the surrounding area. From the living room window of the cottage I could just make out the ferries on their voyage to and from Ireland and it was only a few minutes walk into Holyhead and the Harvest Moon. It was perfect in every way. This little place offered me much more peace and quiet than the house in Stockport and I had found myself very sensitive to city living. I cherished the clean sea air and loving friendships that the island offered.

I continued easily journeying within and regularly going into deep trance. I found my connection with my non-physical guides deepening with each session. In one session I was shown a life in ancient Egypt during which I had been experimenting with consciousness. I felt the cold sarcophagus beneath me as I went deeper into trance. I felt no fear having often, in my Egyptian life, performed this feat to amuse the other initiates undertaking these experiments. This was to be my final initiation. Next moment, I could see myself floating above the whole scene, feeling total peace, knowing that on some other level I had agreed to undertake this experience. I had separated my Egyptian consciousness from my body just a little too long and passed over.

I cannot say for sure this was a past life as it could just as easily have been a future projection. I'm fully aware of my own multi-dimensionality and believe we are all able to tap into any experience we wish to have for whatever reason. My own experiences were usually spontaneous and always brought me closer to understanding myself within the context of existence and spirituality.

EGYPT CALLING

"My soul is from elsewhere, I'm sure of that, and I intend to end up there."
– Rumi

The inner encounter with Egypt left a lasting impression and I knew I had to manifest the money to go there. Soon after, sure enough, the money showed up as it usually does when we have a really deep desire. Les phoned to say we still had a joint insurance policy that could be cashed in giving us a few thousand pounds each. He wanted to book a holiday with his partner and our daughter with his share of the money. I told John my plans to visit Egypt at long last as we had shared a passion for the country when we were together.

As expected, modern-day Egypt is busy, noisy and unkempt. We drove from the port of Alexandria to Cairo past long stretches of unfinished buildings. We learned that if people left the roof off the home they were building they would avoid having to pay taxes.

Seeing the pyramids poking through the modern buildings was surreal. But there they were - majestic structures that had stood the test of time. I was quickly off the coach and rushed to one of the guides standing outside the pyramids. I couldn't hide my disappointment when he said they had just closed for the day. How could this be? My guidance had never failed me. Then it came to me in a flash that I had to go to the Sphinx. The image appeared in my mind very clearly. That was the place I was meant to connect with and a few minutes later, as I stood beneath the giant structure, I went cold from head to toe. Interestingly, I felt the same energy when I stood close to the giant obelisk of the Washington Monument while living in D.C. years before.

I had the sense that my higher self was somehow realigning me with these important places. One of the most powerful sites I ever visited was the Avebury monument in Wiltshire, the largest stone circle in Europe believed to have been erected 4,500 years ago. I've been drawn to visit Avebury many times and I always come away feeling renewed in some way.

On the final day of the trip I visited the Museum of Cairo. The artifacts were awe-inspiring but we had to rush through the exhibits because I was close to fainting from the unbearable heat. I remember noting that the folding bed taken by Tutankhamun on his travels had screw-like fixtures similar to those available in any modern DIY store. Was this more evidence of our multi-dimensionality? The whole visit was exhilarating and I promised myself I would return. On my return to Holyhead, I discovered that my son was coming to live with me for a while. I was totally thrilled to have him come to stay and what was to be a few weeks stay turned into a few years as he began his work as a chef in one of the local seafood restaurants.

JOHN OF GOD

"Faith is a knowledge within the heart, beyond the reach of proof."
– Kahlil Gibran

John and I decided to make a commitment to each other and we married in Anglesey on the summer solstice in 2005. We took our vows in the local registry office and my Mum and Stacey came to celebrate the day. We had a spiritual ceremony in the orchard at Orsedd Isaf where friends had dressed the trees with white ribbons. It was a glorious sunny day and many friends from both Stockport and the island attended. Gwen read the beautiful Ceremony of the Roses and we shared food in the Celtic roundhouse that Roger and Dorothy had built on their land to host spiritual gatherings.

All was going fairly well between us until John started to display his old ways again. He became distant and refused to come out of the cottage for days on end. I began to accept it as the norm and spent my days on the land or at the Harvest Moon. I never spoke of what went on behind closed doors as I wanted to protect John's reputation as a hypnotherapist.

My cousin Maureen, originally from Stockport now lived an hour's drive in Prestatyn and we would often meet up either at her place or ours. She had just returned from a three-week visit to a spiritual retreat in Brazil, home to the spiritual healer Joao de Deus or John of God. She was so enthused by the experience that I went to visit her to find out more about him. I picked up a book she had brought back and once more felt that definitive tingling, really powerful this time. The book was practically shaking in my hand. I knew I had to go. It seemed there was still more of myself to discover.

I headed back to Anglesey that evening and checked flights online. I shared the information with my friends and within weeks, thirteen of us, some from Anglesey and some from Stockport, set off on what was to become the adventure of a lifetime. I was completely unprepared for the magnitude of what was about to unfold.

Shortly before our departure, one of the television channels showed a feature about John of God's healing work. The program showed him entering deep trance and apparently giving over his body and mind to the discarnate spirits of doctors and surgeons who had passed over but wished to be of earthly service. Claiming not to be responsible for the healing, he purported only to be an instrument of God's healing energy.

It felt imperative that I witness channeled healing in order to cast light on my own experiences. When I worked with people, I felt I was somehow 'switching channels'. It wasn't me 'doing' the healing. I was allowing a higher power to use me as its conduit. I wanted to know more about John of God's work in this area. I felt passionate about achieving my potential in this field and was aware of the possibilities of entrainment, the synchronization of a lower vibratory rate to a higher one. This higher vibration, at its peak, is pure Love. I felt sure that I would find some answers in Brazil.

The TV program showed some procedures and when six-inch metal tongs were inserted into a patient's nose, I thought I would pass out. John of God performed both psychic and physical surgeries without administering anesthetic or pain medication. I couldn't wait to visit and hoped I would be able to experience a surgery. Maureen's book said that after initial scanning he would recommend either meditation or an operation.

The day of departure arrived. Ann and Derek met our group at Manchester Airport. Ann was a beautiful woman who had taken tour guests to visit Casa de Dom Inacio for several years since receiving a powerful healing experience while escorting a friend there. We took the eighteen-hour flight to London and Brasilia and boarded the chartered mini-bus that took us on a one-hour drive up to the village of Abadinia. When we finally arrived at the Casa, I was tired but elated. As soon as I put my feet on the ground I could feel a powerful energy pulse pass through me. I later discovered that the place was situated on a foundation of natural quartz crystal, well known for its healing properties. Before even seeing Joao, we were already being affected by the center's vibrations.

We were taken to the place that would be our home for the next three weeks. Former healed visitors who had decided to stay on in service to the community managed the small buildings lining the main street. Our room was very basic but comfortable and all meals were served for the duration of our stay at minimal cost. There was no fee for Joao's healing services.

There were morning and afternoon sessions three times a week. We all sat with eyes closed for three hours enjoying the powerful experience of being among so many people of like mind. When our time came to stand in front of Joao, I immediately felt his powerful presence. There was a male interpreter to translate from his native language of Portuguese. After a minute, I was handed a piece of paper by the interpreter and ushered out of the building where soup was provided. The writing on my paper suggested I bathe under the sacred waterfall before my next session – a task apparently asked of many, including several from our group.

On one of the days we didn't visit the Casa, we explored the surrounding area and found a juice bar where we purchased freshly made drinks and tasty organic food. We spent much time in its walled garden chatting about our experiences or lying happily in one of the bar's hammocks watching huge butterflies flying gracefully and listening to the bird's songs.

I enjoyed every minute at this magical healing place

as did the others in my group. One day during the second week of our stay, I stood in front of Joao for the second time. I was given another piece of paper and told that he would give me a healing operation. It was generally known that if a visitor was under the age of fifty they could request the operation be a physical one. While sitting over our bowl of soup after the session, I discovered that five us had been chosen for surgery. I wanted to experience an actual physical operation in order to develop my knowledge. The others had Joao's group healing during which he would raise his hands and say to the group sitting in front of him, "In the name of Jesus Christ you are all healed".

After their psychic operation, the group returned to their rooms and rested. After the next session those of us who had asked for the physical procedure stood in a row and waited for Joao to attend to each of us. With my eyes closed, I could hear him moving along the row. I could also hear the sound of metal instruments being dropped into the metal bowl his assistant was carrying. Just at the moment I felt his huge presence by my side I began to shake with fear but it was too late to do anything about it by then. I felt his large hand on my shoulder and knew I was about to undergo the nose operation I had watched on the television program! Before I knew it, I felt an instrument enter my nostril but felt nothing further. It was as if I'd been given a local anesthetic of some sort.

Immediately after, I was put into a wheelchair and taken to a nearby recovery room feeling relieved I had come through unscathed. There were beds in the room where my friends were lying. I was handed a cotton swab for my nose and asked to lie down. I asked my cousin in the opposite bed what had happened to him. He had watched while Joao took a scalpel and made a fairly deep incision in his upper stomach area that was later stitched. The five of us had the most extreme experiences.

After a short rest we were taken back to our hotel rooms and advised to drink the provided holy water and stay in bed for the next 24 hours. I was very happy to comply as I'd begun to feel very spaced out. I slept for hours and on awaking could barely see or hear anything. Strangely, I didn't panic at all and just accepted the situation. Two days later I was still in bed unable to move with pain in my left ribcage. I was still unable to see or hear very well and could barely make it to the bathroom without passing out. All the time friends brought me drinks and soup from the Casa. On the third day I finally felt fit enough to join the others down the street at the juice bar where we sat for hours sharing our experiences.

Apparently, the procedure I underwent was one of the most extreme that Joao administered. One of the assistants told me that the nose operation treated up to nine areas in the body simultaneously and that I'd had work done on my spleen. That made sense as it was the area in which I'd felt the most discomfort.

The whole experience was fascinating. For my remaining time there, I had a much closer connection to the unseen world around me and my eyesight and hearing became much more acute. Would I go through it again? Yes! Skeptics claim Joao is deceptive but many thousands of treatments have been filmed and he has been under scientific scrutiny for the many years he has served humanity. My questions regarding the viability of energy healing had been answered.

One day while peeling vegetables for the soup that was made for the visitors, my friend told me she had dreamt of crystals during the night. I was surprised because I had dreamt of them as well. After, we found Joao's assistant sitting on the wall just outside the Casa and shared our dreams. He told my friend she could take some of the Casa's little quartz crystals back home with her to Anglesey. He told me that occasionally Joao would give two master quartz crystals to those whom he felt would benefit and that he would ask him if I could be a recipient.

The next day Joao requested I visit the meditation and prayer room where he prepared himself to go into session each day. I could hardly believe my good fortune as I had wanted to connect with him directly without anyone else in the room. I walked into the small suite where I could see from his wet hair that he had recently showered. There were only a few items there: a chair, flowers and pictures of Jesus. As he walked across the room I could see he was in trance and knew he was already connected with whoever was to do the day's healing work. He was holding two cloth bags with the imprint of Saint Ignatius on them and I guessed that they were the crystals I was to receive. He handed them to me without a single word and I took them and thanked him. He nodded his head and accompanied by his personal assistant, I was soon outside in the sun once again. It was a great honor and a memory I'll never forget.

I was told that the crystals had gender. Male and female, and that I was to pray with them daily and that they would help me stay healthy while I did my healing work. During the afternoon session I sat in front of Joao while the crystals were placed under his chair. The next day I was required to sit in meditation while holding them in my hands. Afterward, his assistant asked me if I had had anything come to mind during my sitting. I had always received images easily so had no problem relating my experience. I'd heard a voice telling me that I was holding the hand of God and then, in my mind's eye, I was approached by a young man using a walking stick and rubbing his leg perhaps indicating he wanted some healing from me.

I was surprised to learn that the young man in my vision was Saint Ignatius himself who, in his early years, had suffered a leg injury in a battle. That day I was given permission to take the crystals home with me when we returned to the UK at the end of the week. I have used the crystals over the years and I treasure them. They have helped me a great deal in my meditations and healing work.

The visit to Brazil was another mind-blowing and life affirming time in my search for healing possibilities.

I came to understand that the more I opened my mind, the more I could receive. I continued to practice my healing work, using the mental images that came even more clearly to me since taking the trip. My visit to Joao de Deus was invaluable not only on a personal healing level but in strengthening my own abilities to work with those who came to me subsequently for help.

TAKING ON TEACHING

"The teacher who is indeed wise does not bid you to enter the house of his wisdom but rather leads you to the threshold of your mind."
– Kahlil Gibran

A few months after I returned home to Anglesey, John complained of feeling unwell and took to sleeping for much of the day. I begged him to see a doctor but he refused. One day we went out for a game of badminton at the local sports centre with my brother who was visiting. As I watched them play I noticed that John was finding it difficult to keep up and the game was cut short. That night he awoke feeling nauseous and suffering from chest pains. I got him into the car and raced twenty miles to the nearest hospital in Bangor where it was confirmed that he was having a heart attack.

After a week in the hospital I brought him back to the cottage. He refused to take the medication he'd been prescribed and became verbally abusive. He would shout at me saying that I had been the cause of his heart attack and that he regretted all the relationships he'd had with the women in his life. I felt his outburst was simply an emotional reaction, continued to care for him, and hoped time would heal him. Two months later, he was feeling better and wanted to return to Stockport. I wanted the best for him and agreed. I offered the cottage to my son and his girlfriend and they eagerly accepted.

Within six weeks we were back in our hometown, living minutes away from my family. We contacted a friend called Costa to see if he might be interested in starting a hypnotherapy school with us in Manchester, an idea discussed a few years before when he and John ran supervision groups in the area.

We met several times with Costa who practised from offices in Chorlton, a suburb of Manchester. Together we co-created a course with a more spiritual approach than was found in conventional hypnotherapy. John had spent most of his career focusing on past lives and Costa already offered a soul retrieval course so we had a good grounding in the areas we wanted to cover. I was more than happy to become student liaison manager that meant I could spend more time on a personal level with the students.

Eventually, with course details in place and the company name and logo agreed upon we submitted our proposal to the Hypnotherapy Association. It was approved and we began our first weekend training soon after running two courses a year with an average of ten students from all walks of life. Some were practicing therapists and some had become interested in the power of the mind through various means.

This was a wonderful time, as we empowered attendees to live full and happy lives. We watched people grow in confidence and many who had been suffering from illness became emotionally and/or physically pain-free. We knew this would have a ripple effect with trainees qualifying and going out into the world to help many others in turn. It was very fulfilling.

Sometimes John and I taught past-life weekends in which I shared examples of deep trance work with the students. In demonstrations I channeled entities that would bring with them words of love and encouragement for the students. This was completely natural for me and I found myself letting go more deeply each time I channeled.

At home, I often found myself alone as John had other family obligations and friends, so I continued my self-development. I often sat with the Brazilian crystals in meditation. On one such occasion I asked for a non-physical guide to come forward to work with me. There had been many of these guides over the years and they would simply leave when the time was right. On this occasion, I clearly heard the name 'Seth'.

Amazed, I wondered if this was the Seth I had read about, the well-known spirit teacher channeled by Jane Roberts and Robert Butts. The answer that came back was affirmative and my heart flooded with the familiar warmth that I felt whenever loving souls came to assist me on my path. My questions about the meaning of life in both the physical and the non-physical realms were answered and I gained reassurance about the unfolding of life. There were many of these sessions until one day it was time for Seth to move out of my mind having given me a greater understanding of reality.

Energetic Blood

"Blood will tell all, but often it tells too much."
– Don Marquis

While advertising our course at a Mind Body Spirit exhibition at Manchester's GMEX Centre, I came across a booth with a large monitor with an image of live blood cells magnified 28,000 times. I learned from the owner that she was promoting Live Blood Analysis, a process developed by Dr Robert Young, a well-published microbiologist who promoted an alkaline diet for wellbeing.

The familiar tingling kicked in and I asked if she would test me. She took a small sterile needle and pressed it into my little finger putting the resulting dot of blood onto a slide for viewing. In a few moments, she asked me what I was doing to get such positive results. I could see that the round cells on the screen were moving freely and the surrounding fluid was clear. I told her that I meditated regularly, ate in moderation and enjoyed a glass of wine and a bit of chocolate occasionally. She told me that whatever I was doing it was obviously the right thing for me.

After the weekend was over, I felt compelled to find out how I could add this technique to my healing toolbox. It instantly illustrated how our thoughts affect us at a cellular level. I found a doctor who was about to run a course in the London area and in no time found myself enrolled along with several others. As the course progressed I knew I would buy a microscope and begin practising immediately.

One day I was asked to be a test subject. I sheepishly went up front and put out my finger. When my blood appeared in the microscope, it looked even healthier than it had at the MBS exhibition. The tutor looked surprised and joked to the class that I must be an alien as he'd never come across such energetic blood. Lunchtime arrived and we ate at a nearby café. On our return we discovered that the lights on the microscope had accidentally been left on, a great opportunity said the tutor, to examine the appearance of blood left outside the body for some time. He was more than surprised to find that my blood was still moving around when it should have deteriorated into stillness. For the rest of the day, I was surrounded by students wanting to know what I did to maintain my health. All I could do was repeat my assertions about moderation, meditation and chocolate.

Two weeks later, having gained my qualification I returned to pick up the microscope I'd ordered. A few days earlier my Mum had had a very bad episode of ill health and I was struggling to come to terms with her suffering. John was also giving me a hard time as he'd done so often in our relationship. Showing me how to set up the microscope, my tutor took another sample of my blood to test. This time, the cells were torpid and almost glued together, a completely different result than my previously healthy readings. The tutor was astonished and asked what was going on in my life to cause such a change.

I shared the reasons with him and he offered me some healing that I gratefully accepted. We then took another blood sample to find it had improved radically. Here was validating scientific proof that our beliefs and thoughts have real power to affect our body's health.

I used the microscope in my practice from that day on helping others in their self-healing. As if I hadn't crammed enough training into my life, I continued my studies adding Colon Hydrotherapy in France, gaining I-ACT (International Association for Colon Hydrotherapy) and Level Two Certification although it's a qualification I've never employed.

THE GATEWAY

*"All that we are is a result of what we have thought ...
What we think we become."*
– Buddha

The number of students enrolling on our courses began
to rise. The rooms in Chorlton were no longer sufficient
for our needs so I looked for larger premises closer to
Stockport in order to have space to do my own work
along with a larger room for training. I found offices in
Hillgate, two miles from our home. It was affordable
and perfect for our purposes. We named it The Gateway,
inspired by two ten-foot tall standing stones on
Anglesey.

I occupied the large front office that housed my
equipment while John used the back office for his
hypnotherapy practice. There was a kitchen and dining
area for the students and a vast teaching room upstairs.
We began working there almost immediately. Costa
continued to practise from his offices in Chorlton and
joined us during the training weekends. Between the

hypnotherapy trainings we ran other self-development courses.

Things went on as normal as they ever were for me. I would usually sit in the teaching room on course weekends. Although I had no desire to teach I loved being part of the process. I never shared the images, colors and non-physical beings I could see around the students and simply accepted them as additional bits of information about each of them. They would tell me that the atmosphere in the room felt different when I was present and I would be asked to return if I ever went to my office. I really enjoyed the interaction with the students and they often found their way to my office in between teaching sessions. They would surround my desk asking me to tell them of my travels and healing experiences. I loved sharing my stories knowing how storytelling can inspire and empower. The tutors weren't too impressed since these visits had a knock-on effect on the training sessions that began to run a bit late.

On training weekends, I would see people for individual work, and became quite used to people turning up at the centre to ask for healings. One particular case involved Anna, a young woman suffering from schizophrenia, who insisted I see her straight away. She said that the angels had told her to come and see me. I have never turned away anyone asking for help so I set up an appointment to see her.

We had a brief conversation before the session started, though this rarely mattered. The energy worked regardless of any words that were exchanged. I asked her to lie down and close her eyes. I changed channels in my mind in order to receive the images I worked with and immediately saw an image of a black snake coiled up in her lower abdomen. By now she was in a deep state of relaxation. I mentally asked this energy if it would like to come out into my waiting hands. Straight away it obeyed and I passed it to one of the non-physical beings at my side. Holding my hands above her I watched as light showered down into the area where the snake had been. Minutes later, Anna sat up. She explained that she'd felt something dark had been taken from her and that the same angels had appeared to tell her everything would be fine now. Weeks later she turned up at my room again looking radiant. She had come to say that since that day she hadn't needed to take any of her medications and she'd found a job after years of being unable to work. I thanked the Star Beings for their loving help and wondered what might be next on the horizon.

During one of our courses I felt drawn to sit next to Polly, one of the female students. This beautiful young woman in her early twenties had a sight impairment that left her partially blind. She had a gentle presence and rarely spoke in the group training. As we spoke about her life she revealed she had practiced Reiki for the past few years. She asked if I might work with her as she wanted to be able to see better, both physically and non-physically. She told me she had been searching far and wide hoping to experience more of the intangible world she had read about in her spiritual training. I was delighted to be of help and agreed to start working together the following weekend. What transpired were several of the most magical sessions I had conducted and resulted in Polly's wish coming true. I loved every minute of our play time together knowing full well that my Star Beings were always at hand and would never fail to assist in whatever was needed at any given moment. With Polly's permission, I have added her story to the postscript of this book.

One night while in a dream state, I heard the word 'resonance' being chanted for what seemed like the whole night. I was shown a picture of waves of color. The next day as I waited for my first appointment to arrive, a woman I had known slightly for a while entered the room. She had attended our meditation nights in the past and consulted John on a few occasions. Her name was Jill. After the session I remembered the dream. Jill is a brilliant artist who hand-dyes small pieces of silk in vibrant colors and stitches them together to make large delicate tapestries. She understood my dream recognizing a piece of her art that matched my description. From that first meeting we became almost inseparable talking often about the Beings of Light that would channel through me often presenting them selves as color. Jill was to become my right arm during the years to follow.

AUSTRALIA

"Though we travel the world over to find the beautiful, we must carry it with us or we find it not."
– Ralph Waldo Emerson.

It was almost Christmas and school was out for the next five weeks. I'd been spending a lot of time on Skype with my old school friend Yvonne in Adelaide who suggested that John and I spend some time with her. We looked for flights straight away and the following week were on our way to see my long-lost friend.

When we met at the airport I realized Yvonne had hardly changed. Her daughter Victoria was now twenty years old and I hadn't set eyes on her since she was a baby. Yvonne's partner Martin was an Australian she had been with for some years.

It was a wonderful and memorable holiday. After spending the first week in Adelaide we all took off in the car for a road trip. First stop was Melbourne and I didn't want to leave again. It had everything. A city with a beach it was such a vibrant and fun place to be. Then we were off again to Sydney which, on my return, I loved as much as Melbourne.

We drove back down the Great Ocean Road. It was stunning, although the temperature was above average for that time of year and we often had to retreat to the car or indoors to keep cool. Yvonne was acclimatised by now but we found the heat almost unbearable.

Of all the Australian cities it was Adelaide that most touched my heart. It was small and very easy to get around, and known as the 'Festival City'. We would meet up either at the harbour or on Glenelg Beach to eat in the evenings. One day we took the short drive out into the Barossa Valley to visit the vineyards. It was lush, serene and beautiful.

We lay in the swimming pool late at night looking up at the impossibly bright stars reminiscing about our schooldays and the paths we had chosen to take. In the intervening years, Yvonne had become interested and well read in spirituality and asked me if I would take her into a past life. We hoped we would discover a time in which we were incarnated together. Sure enough her session revealed that we had both been nuns and inseparable friends. In one moving scene, I was very old and on my deathbed and she was keeping vigil with me until my passing. As usual, it was a mind-expanding experience and more so for Yvonne as it was her first time being regressed.

It was very difficult when it came time to leave knowing we might not get to meet again for a long time. We said our tearful goodbyes and I boarded my return flight to the UK and my office doing what I loved most.

THE INDIAN CONNECTION

"Reach high, for stars lie hidden in your soul. Dream deep, for every dream precedes the goal."
– Pamela Vaull Starr

I telephoned my children often. I was relieved to find they were happy and 'doing their thing' and taking regular holidays abroad with their father or friends. Les had met a much younger woman shortly after I went on my way and, thankfully, had found happiness with her. She wasn't too much older than Stacey and they were more like friends than Step-Mum and daughter. Ashley was still living in the cottage on Anglesey.

My Mum's health was deteriorating. My sisters and brother selflessly attended to her every need, not an easy task with their own children to look after. I visited her at least once a week and talked with her on the phone many nights when she felt most lonely. As long as I could remember my Mum had suffered. She was forever giving herself to anyone who asked. She never really came to terms with the life she had lived. It wasn't easy for any of us to watch what she had to go through.

She was racked with guilt and remorse and it seemed there was nothing any of us could do to relieve her angst.

Around this time, my relationship with John became severely strained, though our dedication to our work held us together. In truth, our relationship should really have been about work. To outsiders it appeared a normal marriage but behind closed doors it was no more than a working partnership. He was becoming increasingly agitated by my views on spirituality and life in general. He would book himself holidays with friends and take off without any discussion. In the meantime, I got on with my work.

One day I received a phone call from a potential client who booked an appointment for the following week. He lived in the Lake District and introduced himself as Andrew. When I asked him who had recommended me, he was vague. As soon as he arrived the following week I felt that we had met somewhere before. He was a lovely, gentle soul.

We started to work together with his presenting problem and within minutes he had discovered a solution. The whole session went well and took about two hours. After the session, I was finished for the day and decided to walk to the train station with him. We talked all the way into the centre of Stockport and found we had many similarities in our understanding of spirituality. I liked this man a lot and by the time we approached the station we'd agreed to stay in touch and swapped phone numbers. As we waved goodbye I couldn't help hoping we would meet again one day in the future.

By the following week I was fully booked with people coming for treatments and had put our encounter in the back of my mind. Then I received another call from Andrew. He told me he felt very well after the session and had found a place inside himself that he never knew existed. I was very happy for him and quickly told him it was his own achievement and that I had only been a guide to help him on his path. Once again we said goodbye and made a promise to keep in touch.

What happened next was something I had heard about but never experienced. Picking up the mail one day before leaving for the office, I opened a handwritten envelope. It contained a card from Andrew depicting a waterfall scene and, stunningly, a cheque for a large sum of money. Inside was written, "Dearest Julie, please accept this from my heart to yours. In your accepting this gift from me, I feel all will move forward for you on your spiritual journey." I called him at once to say I was very grateful for his generous gift but couldn't possibly accept it. He was adamant that I should keep the money, saying he needed to learn how to let go and gift others and my receiving it would enable movement for both of us. I eventually accepted his gift and it provided the much-needed funds to take the next step on my journey.

I began to wonder how Andrew had found me. I had a friend and ex-student who was now a hypnotherapist and osteopath. He had mentioned a client of his by the name of Raj who had often spoken about wanting to meet me. Now I wanted to discover if this man was in some way connected to Andrew. It was all rather mysterious.

I had just returned from a visit to receive Darshan (a blessing) from Mother Meera, an Indian spiritual teacher thought by many to be an avatar. I felt a need to phone my hypnotherapist friend to ask if Raj had been to see him recently and was surprised to hear that he was due that very evening for a treatment. He suggested I come over for a meeting so I drove over to his clinic.

I sat in the treatment room, waiting. When at last a tall dark man with a beaming smile entered the room I knew at once it was Raj. He took one look at me laughed and said, "Ah, at last we meet!" Yes, it was he who had recommended me to Andrew although until that point we had never met. Yet when I asked how he knew of me he just started to laugh again and declined to answer.

After talking together about healing for an hour or so I let him know I had to go. It was getting late and I hadn't eaten for some time. Saying he lived close by in Salford, Raj invited me to share food with him so I accepted thinking I wanted to learn more about this interesting man. Outside, waiting for him, was a chauffeur-driven Bentley alongside another car containing four women. I followed in my car for the five-minute ride to his apartment block.

Entering the apartment, I was hit by the familiar smell of incense and could see that the place had been

turned into a sort of Indian Ashram. There were
pictures of Jesus and Buddha among other spiritual
figures, and a golden Buddha statue stood five feet high
in a corner of the room. There were also a few other
women present, as well as the ones who had arrived in
the car.

Once I had been introduced I was given fresh juice
to drink and invited to speak with him. He said he
would like to guide me on my spiritual path and I
sensed it might be wise to leave as things were getting
stranger by the minute. I thanked him for the drink and
he suggested there was someone interesting I should
meet before I left so I followed him across the hall to the
adjacent apartment. Passing a man dressed in orange
robes standing outside we entered a very large room
with more pictures of Jesus, Buddha and other Masters
on the walls. In front of me sitting cross-legged on a
large settee was an Asian man wearing a yellow silk
tunic. The room was full of people sitting on the floor
some dressed like the monk outside. I was obviously in
the presence of a living spiritual figure.

Somehow, I found myself rushing across the room.
To the surprise of the man's many followers I jumped
onto the settee to give him a hug. Despite this
apparently improper conduct in the presence of a
Master, he had no complaints whatsoever and seemed
to enjoy every minute of it. I felt great warmth coming
from him though he didn't speak a single word
throughout the whole visit. He had an interpreter who
asked me to demonstrate how I channeled energy for

healing. I held my hands over one of the men sitting on the floor. After a few minutes he indicated he'd seen what he wanted to see and I stopped. He called me over again and seemingly pulled a pendant out of thin air that he gave to me. I was told it was a blessing.

After staying a little longer I again sensed it was time to depart. This was all very fascinating but I was becoming a little anxious and, as if I hadn't embarrassed myself enough by the scene on the sofa, I could hardly believe the words that came out of my mouth next. All eyes were upon me, and time seemed to grind to a halt as I blurted out, "I think my chicken will be overdone by now. It's been in the oven for three hours." Not exactly the thing to say to a room full of vegetarian spiritual devotees!

Red-faced, I hurried towards the door. I was told that I would be welcome to visit him anytime. Raj offered me a contact telephone number. He said I had some work to do on myself before my true purpose would unfold and that he would be happy to guide me to that purpose.

I arrived back home to a budgie-sized chicken in the oven. Oh well. At least I had met his Holiness Padmashree Siddhyog Peeth!

TRIP TO LA

"We are all star stuff."
– Carl Sagan

The Gateway was starting to get busier. We were running a self-hypnosis course in the evenings and I'd met Wasyl Kolesnikov, a very talented Tai Chi master and the author of several books on the subject. He agreed to teach at the Centre and we were delighted to add his classes to our offerings.

I received an email from a good friend I'd met in Brazil. He'd been over for a visit the year before when he was going through a particularly difficult time and suggested I visit California to stay with him and help a friend of his who needed healing. I was accustomed to traveling far and wide to people's homes to help them and this invitation would take me back to my favorite part of the world. I had stayed in Florida when I was eighteen and the year in Washington, DC had never left my heart. Wherever I went, I loved everyone I met but there was something special about American people that

I resonated with. Above all, I found them very easy to be with.

I booked a flight to Los Angeles for the three weeks before Christmas. I stayed overnight in a hotel close to the airport and the next morning picked up my rental car and made the thirty-minute drive along Pacific Coast Highway to the address I had been given in Malibu. The house was unique in my experience with ocean and coastline views. I was excited to be working in such a beautiful environment. My friends and I spent the whole night catching up on events since our trip to Brazil. They had returned for a second visit after having such an amazing time on their first.

In the three weeks I was there I did everything I could imagine and more. I loved Sunday mornings at the Paramahansa Yogananda temple followed by breakfast on the Third Street Promenade where the street performers played on weekends. I took sightseeing tours to Universal Studios and Disneyland where my inner child played to her heart's content.

I was asked to do several healing sessions during my stay and was surprised to find increased intensity and effectiveness. People reported being aware of the Beings that worked with me and feeling physical hands on the organs that needed work. It caused quite a stir in the area and word spread quickly. People in need of healing appeared in increasing numbers.

A mother brought her 1½-year-old girl to see me. A beautiful ethereal child, she had never really connected with the earth plane and was under the care of five therapists. She was a twin and her sister was completely adjusted. I could see how disturbing her situation was for the mother and the child. The child threw herself all over the place and her eyes were unable to focus on anything.

I guided them both into one of the rooms where I could work in peace. It was difficult to talk as the child had to be almost pinned down to stop her falling onto the floor. My heart went out to her mother. She had tried everything and had very little hope. I told her I was simply a channel of the energies worked through. This lovely lady had never heard of this type of healing but was willing to give anything a try.

I asked her to lie down next to her daughter and within seconds she entered a state of deep relaxation. I held my hands above the little girl's eyes and almost immediately she looked straight into mine. It was as though she recognized something in me and she relaxed and became totally still. As I continued to hold my hands in this way I saw images of her playing in the garden. After about ten minutes my hands relaxed and the child stayed where she was. At the same moment her mother came awake and started crying explaining she knew her little girl was going to be fine having seen in her mind's eye the child playing in their garden. We talked a little and she picked up her little girl who was still very calm. She hadn't seen her daughter so at peace since she'd been born.

During my time in LA, I was able to help many people. Unwittingly, I became a bit of a celebrity healer in the area and met with a television talk show host who asked if I would appear on her show. I've never been comfortable with this sort of attention so avoided any commitment. I hadn't expected to do so much healing work but had loved every minute of my time there. My beautiful friends had taken such good care of me and I was grateful for their warm hospitality.

SPIRIT SURGERY

"For the wise man looks into space and he knows there is no limit to dimensions."
— Lao Tzu

When I arrived home, I went into the office for the start of a past life weekend. I was still in California mode and feeling very bright indeed. The students were eager to hear about my healing experiences and I loved sharing them. In the tearoom that morning attentive students surrounded me. As always, I enjoyed encouraging others to understand what can be achieved when we allow ourselves to release our grip on life and go with the flow.

While I spoke, Sue, one of the students, kept to the back of the room as if she was afraid of something. We did our normal teaching day and things were going very well. Students always loved these weekends finding the subject of past lives fascinating. On the second day I went into my trance work sitting at the front of the class with my eyes closed and feeling the love flowing from my heart. After the session was over I felt a non-physical presence still with me and said out loud, "Is there someone in the room who would like some healing?" I surprised myself with this as it wasn't something I'd done in previous courses.

Sue shot her arm up and cried out, "I didn't do that. Something just lifted my arm for me!" She looked surprised as did the rest of the class. I asked again if she wanted some healing and she said yes. I walked across the room, still in trance, to stand next to her. All the other students watched and waited for what was to come next.

I held my hands about a foot away from her. One hand was facing her chest and the other facing her back. No one was prepared for what happened next. Sue and the chair she was sitting on began to shake. She started to look hot and slightly uncomfortable. I couldn't move my hands an inch. I asked if she was OK and she said yes and gave me permission to continue with the healing. After about five minutes, I felt my hands release. She looked shocked and said that her experience had been so momentous that she had to go home immediately to try to assimilate it.

Sue telephoned that evening. She explained she had felt hands enter her chest and correct a heart problem she was aware of but hadn't divulged on her course application form. She had also mentally witnessed the operation. On returning home she measured her breathing on the device she regularly used, to find it had improved considerably.

Some of the other students came to me to let me

know that when I touched them they felt as if electricity was shooting through them that I was unaware of most of the time. I was simply reaching out from one heart to another.

MUM

"Death is the greatest illusion of all."
– Osho Rajneesh

Life moved on. Stacey was doing well at college where she was taking primary school teaching qualifications while working in a nursery school. Ashley was also thriving in his career as a chef, living and working in Beaumaris, a quaint seaside town on the Isle of Anglesey.

Mum's mobility, however, was becoming more problematic. Over the years she had broken many bones in falls including a hip fracture that hospitalized her for seven weeks. We did everything we could for her but she was now using alcohol to medicate herself. She was terrified of prescription drugs and said drink was a much better form of painkiller. Whenever I visited her there would always be a house full of family and friends around her. She was loved more than she knew.

It was November 2007. My sister phoned to say that Mum had been found lying on her hall floor after falling and breaking her hip again. I was devastated being on the other side of the world in Australia with my son who had come out on a working visa. I knew she couldn't possibly keep on surviving these falls. She weighed only about six stone. She was taken into Stepping Hill Hospital in Stockport for a hip operation though her blood alcohol level was too high and they had to operate using a lowered dose of anesthetic. After the operation, she was not doing well. I began my trip home and telephoned between each flight to see how she was doing. My sister told me she wasn't going to make it this time but wouldn't let go until I was there. She kept crying out, "Where's Julie?"

At Manchester Airport, I told Immigration the situation and they graciously allowed me straight through. I grabbed the first taxi, arrived at her hospital room, and broke down when I saw the state she was in. She was clearly only hours from leaving this world and looked frail, battered and bruised. My sister told me that one of the doctors on call that evening hadn't seen the report requesting no resuscitation and had gone ahead.

The rest of the family went home that night to get some rest as they had been with Mum constantly. I sat in silence with her and whispered how much I loved her. My Mum had loved Jesus all her life so I put a photo of him I had brought by her side. I think Jesus would have been happy if Mum had loved herself too. I repeated to her that he would be there to take her and to look for him in her mind. It was the early hours of the morning when I felt her spirit leave even though the oxygen pump was still pumping away. It was heartbreaking sitting with her, remembering all the hard times she had gone through. The nurse came into the room at 7 am and switched off the machine. I watched the monitor as it flat-lined. Mum was now at peace, thank God.

STAR BEINGS

"We come spinning out of nothingness, scattering stars like dust."
— Rumi

It was March 2008, shortly after Mum's passing. My life with John wasn't getting any easier. I knew that everything was once again falling away and I wondered how much longer our relationship could last. We were hardly ever in each other's presence and he had booked yet another holiday for himself.

I sat quietly, went within and felt the sensations that usually presaged an information download. I needed a deeper understanding of my life path and the work I was doing. I had recently felt that the Beings of Light who I'd been aware of all my life, were trying to make themselves known to me in a more profound way.

I clearly remember feeling as if I was being enveloped by one of the familiar energies that worked through me. After some time in silence, I found myself going far deeper than ever before. I had no fear whatsoever of this process as it had become part of my life. This time, however I was almost catatonic and could barely return to waking consciousness. I felt as though I was being gently pinned down and felt enormous feelings of love in my heart.

When I did finally rouse myself I could hardly move. I stayed with the feelings and continued to rest but was unable to move far from my bed for days. I called out to whatever or whoever was working through me. In trance I picked up the pen and paper that I kept on the bedside table and began to write:

"We are inter-dimensional beings of color, light and sound. We have come to assist you in the cellular changes. You are receiving our communication to work with you, through you, as you."

What was this? I hadn't heard anything quite as definitive before.

"Have faith and know why you are here. Be at peace with yourself. This will help with receiving this information. Your body's electrical circuitry is being rewired. All is well. There is much erasing of past conditioning to be done. This can feel temporarily disorienting. We are what you perceive us to be. You are now awakening to your true identity. We have helped you remember your purpose for being here. Remain open to our communication and we will not fail you. Through the light and information channels you will also help others remember. We are all one."

For the rest of the day I felt like I was walking between worlds. I was very tired but elated at the same time. I wondered if this would continue. The next day I sat down with pen and paper and sure enough the presence was there again.

"Greetings. Use the dimensional library. We will guide you to all the information that you require at any given moment. The information will be given from this point on and will benefit all who ask for guidance. You will experience more in this space. Be at ease as all is contained within and all can be viewed for the greater benefit of mankind. Thank you for trusting in your own intuition. Enjoy your blossoming. In your earthly experience many can receive from your love and openness. You are the keeper. Feel the Christ upon the breath of the heart to guide you in these times."

I sat down in silence trying to absorb what was flowing through me. What did it mean? The feeling of love while I was writing was so intense I couldn't wait until our next time together.

Every day I would feel their presence guiding me. Who were 'they'? They had always been there. Of that I was certain. The words would come into my mind as though they were talking to me telepathically. I asked where they were from and whether I could name them.

"We are what you perceive us to be. If you wish to name us then so be it, although in naming us you will define us and in that there will be limitation."

"We are a group consciousness that has walked the human path. We assist in your awakening for it is time to share on your planet. Know that there is nothing to hold onto. In the penning of these words lies your own truth."

They were my Star Beings. I had no need to try to escape this world. They were with me all the time. I had found my answers and they were here inside me. It seems everything is within us. Our soul will guide us to all we seek. It was always that simple. The great Masters, in their times incarnated to share this truth with us.

Those of us alive today have chosen to be here to assist in our return to awareness and we are the ones we have been waiting for. Only by our own thoughts and actions can we make this world a better place and at no other time has it been so essential that we demonstrate our love for one another and all of life. Our bodies are becoming lighter and we are coming closer to Spirit. If we can let go of fear we will discover all the love we have ever sought.

LUMINARIES

"All you need is love."
– John Lennon

I had been seeing a lot of my loving friend Jill who had been my rock during the previous year. I don't know how I would have gotten through it all without her. She selflessly put her own needs aside while she assisted me in my breaking free. We were still almost inseparable, sharing our spiritual path together.

One morning I awoke with that old familiar feeling and the usual message to take the next step on my journey. I logged on to the web, did a search, and found a Mastery Course that coincided with the center's three-week break. It was located in Hamburg, Germany, a place I'd never visited. The list of speakers included many of the visionaries whose books I had read and greatly admired, including Gregg Braden, Masaru Emoto and Irvin Laszlo.

Dr Eric Pearl, author of *The Reconnection*, led the first weekend. I reserved places for Jill and I and we stayed at the Intercontinental Hotel for ten days. The

whole conference focused on healing and the power of
the mind and I was so excited to be able to meet with
these leaders in conscious evolution.

The hotel was a short walk across the park from the
Hamburg Conference Centre. On arrival we were given
our name badges and went to the auditorium where we
joined some 300 attendees. I sat next to a husband and
wife from Sweden who were medical doctors and used
Reiki in their practice. We spoke with an eclectic mix of
people who shared a great interest in human potential.

The atmosphere was electric. Eric Pearl spoke on
Reconnective Healing, the modality he had developed to
reconnect us to the universe and our own essence
through a new set of healing frequencies. During that
fun-filled weekend, we thoroughly enjoyed practising
his new technique and made the commitment to receive
a personal Reconnection while we were there. The
process was so powerful that we needed to stay in bed
the following morning. As with all healing modalities
there can be a healing crisis after treatment and the
presenting symptoms may get worse before they get
better.

The days flew by. One evening we had dinner on a
cruise boat with the conference speakers. When we were
seated for our meal I noticed the Japanese author,
Masaru Emoto, sitting a couple of tables away. I found
myself staring at him watching as he and his interpreter
chatted away. The man sitting beside me asked if I had
read Dr Emoto's books. I replied that I had and that
they had influenced my work greatly and that I'd gone

on to train with a dark field microscope like the one Dr Emoto used with his water crystals.

After reading Dr. Emoto, I'd been deeply affected by his conclusions that clearly demonstrated how our thoughts affect our lives. In one of his early experiments he placed a glass of water on a piece of paper on which was written the word 'love', and another on paper containing the word 'hate'. He then froze the water and viewed the ice crystals under his microscope. The crystals exposed to the word 'love' were beautiful and symmetrical while the others were disfigured and incomplete. Keeping in mind that the human body is composed of at least 60% water, Dr Emoto's work shows that what we think has profound implications not only for our health and wellbeing but for the planet as well.

Before I knew it my neighbor had dashed over to talk with him and I was surprised to see Dr. Emoto get up and approach our table. He gestured to ask if he and his interpreter could sit with us and handed me his card. We discussed the microscope connection and I told him that when I looked at blood that was mostly water, I felt we were both seeing the same results – real evidence that our thoughts created our reality. We joked together and shared a few ideas. After the meal we said our goodbyes and I promised myself I would email him on my return home.

Masaru Emoto is a being full of light and laughter and clearly transmits the loving message he teaches. I'm forever grateful I had the good fortune to meet him.

That evening I met not one but two human beings who had beautiful auras of love and compassion. Jill and I had danced the night away and were about to leave for our hotel when I noticed an elderly gentleman standing by the door. He seemed to have some special quality and I felt I had to speak with him. I dashed over and found myself taking hold of his hands. He smiled and held on to mine. I said, "You are one of the most beautiful human beings I have ever encountered and I just had to let you know. I hope you don't mind." He gave me a huge smile and replied that he was thrilled and that I too was beautiful. I had no idea who he was until the next day at the conference when he was introduced. It was Ervin Laszlo, the great evolutionary theorist and two-time Nobel Peace Prize nominee. Those few minutes holding his hands left an impression that has stayed with me to this day. What an honor to have spent time with this gentle man. He stood out so clearly that evening in a noisy room full of partygoers.

We were on our way home having had one of the best evenings we could remember. Once I had recovered from the flight, I knew I wanted to learn The Reconnection. I had been told in Hamburg that Eric would soon be running a training in Greece and a week later Jill and I were on a flight to Athens. It was a very intense and noisy experience with 150 people from many countries and their interpreters. Despite the chaos, I wouldn't have missed it for the world and five days later we left Athens with certification in hand.

The whole Reconnection process felt very natural to

me. I felt as if I had done this work before in another place and time. While attending the conference in Hamburg I had the opportunity to approach Eric. I dearly wanted to speak with him about the Star Beings but he was preoccupied and I didn't want to trouble him. I managed to say I thought he was doing a marvelous job of sharing his information with us and he thanked me and hurried on.

Although I value the method I was taught by Eric, I had no choice but to continue on in my healing journey. I was compelled to reach my full potential, and so on I went holding onto nothing as my Star Beings had advised.

ALONE AGAIN

"The soul that sees beauty may sometimes walk alone."
– Johann Wolfgang Von Goethe

Back home, I found there was no way to keep my relationship together. It was time to leave. The lease on The Gateway was due to expire at the end of the month and we made the decision to close down. John was not willing to give up our little apartment and made things so uncomfortable that I decided to move in with Jill until I could get my life together. I was still being asked to do my work traveling around the country although my heart was still drawn to Anglesey. I eventually headed back there.

    I didn't have a clue how I might find a place to live. What money I had would pay for a year's rent at the outside. I was offered a caravan to live in on Orsedd Isaf. I accepted, and couldn't thank Roger and Dorothy enough. For the second time in my life these wonderful people came through for me. I was shaken by my situation but knew I had to surrender and keep going with the flow. Life in the past had always worked out and I had to continue to trust as my Star Beings had reminded me so often.

I carried on with my sessions on the island and many clients had extraordinary and powerful experiences. A few people who came into my presence would almost instantly go into deep trance and fall to the floor. At the time I really couldn't understand what was happening or why. Even when visiting cafes or shops people would stare at me or approach me saying that they thought they knew me. It was all a bit strange and I didn't know what to expect next. In my local coffee shop, I touched the manager one day and he felt a massive surge of energy rush down his spine. This was happening seemingly without any intent or effort on my part.

I wanted to rest but felt I had an obligation to continue while people were receiving these healing effects. Then Jane telephoned me. A freelance photographer from the south of England, she had heard about my work on the island. She had fallen onto a glass coffee table at a party in London hitting her head with resulting brain trauma. Nothing more could be done by the medical professionals and she had gone into retreat. Almost immediately, I heard my guides urging me to travel to her home to do some healing. I offered my help and Jane accepted. Within the week Jill and I were driving to her cottage.

Jane made up the spare room for us and baked a delicious treacle tart. We chatted for much of the evening and arranged to do some healing the following day. After breakfast, we set up the treatment bed and started the session. I did my usual mental channel switching and waited for the images to present themselves. I watched as Jane's head was held by one of the Star Beings and at that moment a tear ran down her face. Another Being oversaw the work as I was handed several long pointed instruments to operate on her head injury. It was all done fairly quickly and matter-of-factly as usual.

Jane mentally saw every detail of the process and her account of it is included at the end of this book. After the session, she described the three Star Beings working with me, the pointy tools and other things that had occurred during her treatment. It was obvious that her speech that had been affected by the accident had become clearer. After she rested for a while, the bump that was present at the start of her session was gone. The next morning we worked a little more and were soon back in the car and on our way home. My ever-loving Star Beings had come through, yet again.

Sedona

"All the world's a stage..."
– William Shakespeare

After living on the island for three months, I knew it was time to return to Stockport to look for an affordable place to live. I continued to see people when I could but for the first time ever, I felt drained.

I called Raj, the man whose apartment I had visited in Salford. He seemed to expect my call and thanked me for contacting him. I explained I had been through a lot of changes and was very tired. He asked if I would allow him to guide me on the next part of my journey and told me that I had much more to do in the future and that I had to improve my physical health for that to happen. I agreed to go to his Ashram in London for a few days and a car was sent to pick me up the following day. I asked if Jill might join me as we rarely went anywhere without each other. He agreed.

We arrived at his home and were shown to our room. Downstairs, people were busy preparing vegan food for the evening meal and I immediately felt comfortable. Seven or so people were staying at the house and many other visitors arrived most evenings for the meditation sessions. Later that morning I went into the meditation room to meet my host. We talked about the path of self-discovery and of my journey.

We were taken to Covent Garden for more delicious vegan food. Over our meal Raj invited me to India where he said I would meet many spiritual beings. It was time, he said, for me to take this journey and he would provide everything I needed. It was a country I had always wanted to visit although I was actually a bit more interested in Tibet.

Before I knew it, we were in the passport office applying for visas to travel six weeks later. In the meantime, I was advised to visit a Chinese herbalist to cleanse my body and undergo massage. I stayed at the house for a few days sitting in meditation and helping prepare the food. I had a lovely time and felt very relaxed by the time I returned home. I was grateful for the help.

I kept in touch by phone regarding our travel plans and promised to return for more meditation when I could but as the weeks went on I realised I couldn't make the commitment to go. I felt it wasn't the right time to make the trip and called Raj to let him know. He was surprised by my decision and said that we could postpone it until I felt ready to go. I never did make that trip.

Sedona, Arizona was the place that really called me. I had heard a great deal about the town over the years and knew it was a high frequency area. Jill and Sarjana, my long-time friend who'd initiated me into Reiki, jumped at the chance to join me. I rang Raj to let him know about my plans and he advised me to sit still. He tried everything to talk me out of it but I said that I always followed my own guidance, had to make the trip, and off we went.

We landed at Phoenix Airport and rented a car, then drove to Scottsdale where we spent two nights before driving the two hours into Sedona. We took our time and loved the scenery. It was so different from anything we had encountered in the past. On arrival, the first thing we saw was Sedona's massive red rock formations. To me, they were huge cathedrals of spirit. I almost burst into tears at the long-awaited sight of them and felt like I had come home.

We drove down the main street with its beautiful art galleries, shops and cafes. Everywhere we looked there were spiritual offerings - Tarot readings, numerologists, healing centers. I felt in my element here. We drove on through the main village until we found the most wonderful log cabins for rent. The front of our cabin overlooked the red rocks and we had a huge balcony to sit on. Eagles circled welcoming us and we looked down onto the bubbling creek below. It was perfect. That first night we lit a log fire, cooked a meal together and settled in.

The next morning we drove into town to explore. We discovered night trips to the Nevada desert to view the UFOs that the area was famous for were being offered. We didn't have to book that tour because after a few nights in our cabin, Sarjana and I witnessed one of the starships close up while sitting on the verandah. We laughed to ourselves as the silver cigar-shaped ship coasted by at low speed. We felt for Jill who had missed it as she had been in her room sleeping at the time.

That first morning, after eating at one of the cafes, we walked into a small healing center tucked away on a back street. The shop window was filled with crystals and colorful artifacts. I turned around and almost bumped into a woman and was hit with the tingling energy that always seemed to precede something meaningful in my life. As we looked into each other's eyes I instantly recognized her face although I had never met her before. She smiled and introduced herself as Thea. She had been living in the area for some years and rented a property overlooking one of the majestic red rock outcroppings.

What she said next almost floored me. "You do not need to visit India. There is someone in your life that wants to take you to meet the Enlightened Ones. You have already been there in your past lives." I told her she was amazingly accurate and explained how we'd just arrived at Sedona instead of going to India.

We were invited to Thea's home and talked for some time about my journey and where I wanted to be. She intuited that I was experiencing uncomfortable burning sensations in my throat area and said that I had been implanted with a program that was holding me back in my life. She offered to energetically remove it for me and I asked her to please proceed. I felt myself wanting to cough as she recited loving words during the healing session. I felt very well after the treatment and thanked her. As we left she gave me a copy of her book that detailed her own spiritual journey saying it might ring some bells for me. (Ivie, Thea. Transcending Illusion. Ascension Publishing Company, 2007.) As we parted, she extended an invitation to return and live with her and her friends if I wanted to. We exchanged phone numbers and emails and promised to stay in touch.

We met many like-minded people in Sedona. It was a very loving place where I felt very close to my Star Family. We thought seriously about returning to start a healing center of our own and even viewed a ranch at the base of Bell Rock, the huge rock formation near the village of Oak Creek.

I wanted the girls to meet my Los Angeles buddies so a few days later we packed the car and made the exhilarating nine-hour drive across the desert. On arrival we called my good friend Kyle. It had been some time since we'd connected with each other and we had so much to catch up on. As we shared what had been happening in our lives, Kyle stopped mid-sentence and said, "I'm not sure why I'm saying this, but I really think it would be a good idea if you dropped my father an email explaining your healing work." He wrote an address down for me and I said I'd write once I was back in the UK. We said our goodbyes and walked back to our Marina Del Rey hotel. We'd missed my other friend who was away working in Hawaii, so we spent the rest of the visit doing the usual tourist thing before taking the long drive back to Sedona.

On the way back to town we decided to take a side trip to the Grand Canyon and booked a flight out of the tiny airport that was positioned at the top of town. The pilot of the small Cessna we were about to board told us the weather didn't look too promising but he would take us across anyway. The aircraft was so small that it just seated the four of us comfortably.

It took us 45 minutes to reach the landing spot by the Canyon, which took our breath away when we saw its amazing size. From there we jumped into a helicopter that dropped us down into the Canyon where we took a boat ride along the river. We were just about to go for lunch when our guide decided the trip would have to be cut short due to the worsening weather so we were soon back in the Cessna flying back to Sedona. The pilot warned us it would be a rough ride but we had to get back and had no choice in the matter. Halfway back we hit a storm. The tiny plane was tossed around the sky and I couldn't believe we stayed aloft. While Jill was busy throwing up, Sarjana and I sat facing each other in frozen silence. There was nothing we could do but 'let go and let God'.

The pilot circled the landing strip three times trying to manage the high winds and twice the wing of the plane nearly crashed into the ground. On the third attempt we finally screeched down. Once firmly on the tarmac he told us he'd lost two passengers and a pilot three weeks earlier in less violent winds. It turned out he was the airport's owner and the most skilled of all the pilots. We almost lost our lives that day but the thing I'll never forget was the strange feeling that I was outside myself observing the whole ordeal. It was the nearest I have ever come to dying in this lifetime.

We soon recovered and even managed to laugh at the situation we had gotten into. We spent most evenings by the log fire sharing food and wine and reviewing the day's experiences. We all agreed we were the happiest we'd been in a long time. On our last day we discovered a magical labyrinth of tiny craft shops displaying Native American art and jewelry and musicians playing in the courtyards. We were mesmerized by its beauty and still talk about the healing love we felt there.

Our time in Sedona was exhilarating and made more so by our Near Death Experience. We all loved the place and agreed that we would return as soon as we were able.

LOVE

"Lovers don't finally meet somewhere. They're in each other all along."
– Rumi

Back in Stockport, Jill and I decided we were going to return to Sedona for a six-month stay. Jill would take samples of her art for the many local galleries that had expressed interest in her work while I had been encouraged to set up a meditation group in the area. We were very happy about returning to what felt like home. Though we were only permitted to stay for six months we felt it was worth it. I told my children about my plans. They knew my relationship with John was over and by now they were accustomed to me running around the planet. They didn't really know much about what I did and whenever I tried to explain it to them they would become irritable and say, "Oh, Mum, why don't you just get a nice shop job and settle down?" In the end I stopped trying.

One morning I was eating my usual breakfast of fruit and yoghurt when my conversation with Kyle came to mind. I went to find his father Jeff's email address and, sitting at the computer, tuned in to him before writing. Almost immediately I felt the familiar warmth in my heart that always came when meeting someone with great spiritual energy. I wrote, explaining that Kyle had suggested I contacted him and Jeff responded straight away. We agreed to talk through Skype so we could speak face to face.

I found that we had much to share. When I first saw his gentle, loving face I felt completely at ease, almost as if I had met a friend I had known for many years. I found he lived in an area of California called Ojai and was the editor of New Paradigm Digest, an online blog on emerging sustainable culture. After our conversation, I took a deeper look into Jeff's work and discovered an amazing resource of hope, linking visionary people and projects making positive change in the world. I felt in tune with what Jeff was communicating, appreciating the global impact of his work, and wished that maybe one day I too could reach out to many more people with my work.

As time went on I turned to Jeff for advice in times of need. He was always there with loving guidance. He has been a constant encouragement to my work and in my finally writing this book after much doubt and prevarication. Without this genuinely kind and loving man there would be no book at all. I simply love him and the work he is doing tirelessly for the planet without ego or need for recognition.

BREAKING FREE

It was May 11, 2010, the day before my son's 28th birthday. He and his girlfriend were expecting their first child the following August. He was working as a chef in the local bar and I stopped by his workplace to drop off a birthday card and present. I rarely, if ever, went into bars but that day it was necessary to catch up with him.

As I walked toward my son I noticed a man sitting by himself. I felt drawn to his presence. It was the same feeling of inevitability I'd had so many times in the past, though totally unexpected in this place. I inquired who he was and Ashley described him as a really nice man who visited the bar occasionally to watch football. Ash and I went outside to sit in the sun and the guy followed us out looking over at me as my son and I chatted. Soon it was time for Ashley to return to the kitchen so we said goodbye and I headed out to the car. I was about to drive away when I found I couldn't move. My mobile phone rang and I answered it to hear my son say that the man I'd noticed had asked for my number. I gave him permission to pass it on and within minutes he phoned while I was still sitting in the car park.

We met for coffee a few days later. He introduced himself as James. I looked into his eyes and out of the blue I sensed I had met the love I had been seeking all my life. As the conversation progressed he told me he had prayed that he would one day meet me again and marry me. I looked at him in complete surprise. He took hold of my hand and told me, "You won't remember me, but I've been in love with you since I first set eyes on you at school."

129

James told me he'd spent all his school years wishing I would speak to him. Thinking back, I remembered the younger boys that used to follow me around. They were in the third year when I was a fifth-year pupil and my friends and I were much too aloof to mix with such youngsters. He had been the boy who'd walked into the supermarket where I worked trying to get up the courage to ask me out. I remembered the occasion and his being a tall dark-haired 15-year-old, but I had no idea about the crush he was secretly carrying. He'd quickly become embarrassed at his own shyness and walked out after only a few minutes' conversation. I never gave him a second thought. I was on my own journey and he was on his.

Now here we were, sitting together 33 years later. I was seeing a mature, handsome man who had been through many life experiences of his own though they were very different from mine. Here, for the first time, was love at first sight with a man who was everything I had ever dreamed of. We shared memories and dreams and laughed for most of the rest of the day. Within a week we had moved in together and two years later we have rarely left each other's side. I love James with all my heart. James is my knight in shining armor. I believe that when we accept and love ourselves our outer world reflects back to us everything we wish for.

Life isn't always easy. Sometimes it brings us great pain but somehow we survive. When we visualize our preferred future, work toward it, let go and allow it, our world can be transformed and a new one manifested. I am blessed and thankful to have met every person in my life. Each and every one of them has brought me closer to myself. All that I have held on the screen of my mind has manifested for me whether it be good or bad and because of this, today I am very careful of the thoughts I keep.

Walking Away

"When you go into the space of nothingness, everything becomes known."
– Buddha

Not long after James and my reunion, my London friend and guide Raj asked if I would return to the Ashram; I took James to introduce him to my way of life. We spent a few days in meditation and Raj wanted to know if my choice to go to Arizona rather than India had enriched me. I said it undoubtedly had and that Arizona, out of all the places I had visited, felt like my true home on this planet. He told me that I would return one day to do my work.

My lifestyle was completely alien to James, who had a strong Catholic upbringing and teaches in a Catholic school. One day we visited a Chinese doctor for cleansing and strengthening herbs and returned to the house to meet with a group of visiting Maori healers. After sharing food we accepted their offer of a traditional treatment. We received deep massage while listening to them sing and play their guitars.

The evening was a complete eye-opener for James who had never experienced any form of healing. On previous visits to the ashram I'd met many healers including one man who had only recently left his Tibetan mountains for the first time. It was a real treat having him read my future. He took my hand and read my palm telling me that my life was surely that of a healer and that I would live to a ripe old age!

The next day we were on our way back to our home in Stockport. James was curious why Raj wanted to help and what the outcome of my training might be. I enjoyed experiencing the way of life in the Ashram. I really didn't know why or what the outcome would be. I just trusted it would be for my highest good.

Soon after our return Jill telephoned me to say that she had heard about a talk being given on our awakening consciousness at Saint James's Church in Piccadilly, London and that it would be an interesting day out for us. I had always wanted to visit Saint James's as I had seen advertisements for many interesting speakers there over the years. I immediately told Jill to make the booking.

We did the usual sightseeing during the day and finally headed to the talk that began at 7pm.

When we walked into the wonderful building my eyes went straight to the massive stained glass windows in front of me. I was almost struck down with the beauty of them. My legs went weak and walking was difficult.

On our way to our seats, we started a conversation with a woman who told us she often attended the talks there. She introduced herself to me as Esther Fieldgrass. I felt her loving presence straight away. After our brief conversation she handed me her card and asked if I would give her a call the following day. The whole day and evening talk had been wonderful but by the end of the evening, Jill and I were both very tired and couldn't wait to board the train back to Stockport.

The next day I called Esther who was pleased that I had decided to call her and told me she had been completely blown away by the energy that came through me that evening, as had the two personal assistants she'd been sitting with. I suggested to her that many people across the planet have the same energy flowing through them and that I didn't know what to do with it other than help each person that asked me for healing in the moment. Then to my surprise she asked me where in the world I would like to live to do my work as she was able to provide the funds to enable that to happen.

She invited me to London to talk with her about my work and how to put it to the best use. Days later Jill and I had dinner with Esther and she offered to promote my work on the London Mind, Body & Spirit circuit. I was very grateful and knew it was an opportunity to be of service in a greater way. We also talked about holding group sessions and she proposed that I work out of her London clinics. It all seemed very positive so I agreed to return a few weeks later when she had gathered some people for a healing circle.

I returned to London with James, this time hoping he might be able to shed some light on why so many people wanted to do something with my energy work and why so many of them couldn't quite grasp what to do with it when they finally met me in person. I was becoming exhausted in moving toward what I thought was the right thing to do with my life. James and I found a very nice hotel in Kensington and booked in for a three-day stay. I led the healing circle that Esther had kindly organised to see if it might generate clients for personal healing sessions, which it did.

For the following two days, I conducted my healing sessions from her state-of-the-art Medispa clinic in Chelsea. Although Esther did her very best to help accommodate my every need, my guides urged me to once again move on. Like many other times in my life when I had encountered loving people who were prepared to help me with what I needed, I knew I had to keep moving forward on my path. I am so very grateful to Esther for providing that wonderful opportunity.

ILLNESS AND PEACE

"Be grateful for whoever comes, because each has been sent as a guide from beyond."
– Rumi

A few weeks later Les, the father of my children, suffered a massive heart attack and died suddenly at the age of 52. For as long as I can remember Les had been terrified of passing the same way as his own father Bob had. He too was 52 when his heart failed. My whole world was thrown into chaos. My children went into severe shock. My grandson Blake wasn't quite a year old. How could this be? Les had been so full of life.

My children wanted little to do with me. I was the one who had abandoned the relationship. I had to step back.

The day of the funeral was difficult. Before the funeral I was summoned by Les's brother, wife, and my children to let me know that Les had named me executor of his will. This wasn't news to me as Les and I had agreed that if anything should happen to him, only I, their mother, would truly have the children's best interests at heart. I was shouted down until, in tears, I handed over the executorship.

During the funeral, I could only watch from the rear of the chapel as my daughter in her grief read out a beautiful poem about her father which contained a clear statement that the two of them felt they had no parents now.

I had been denied the gift of being close to them in their darkest hour. It was unbelievably painful to sit among people with whom I had shared my whole life and have them feel this way about me.

I walked away knowing that Les wanted nothing more at this time than for me to watch over them.

After Les's passing, Rosie, our little dog came to live with me. She was thirteen years old now and I had missed her and her companion, Bob dearly over the years. Bob had passed away at 15, just before Les passed.

I wasn't coping well with the situation and the way it had been handled. I thought I was beyond this sort of pain. After ten years of missing my children and the loss of my mother I thought there could be nothing more painful to deal with but I was wrong. I asked James if we could go away to Anglesey while this cleared. I prayed that my children would come to understand my love for them one day. I realized how difficult it was for them to have a mother like me. My spiritual life was all-consuming and they had to live with the constant reminder that this was what had led me away from them and their view of family life.

My health was at a low point. I knew I was creating illness but I had to work things out for myself as I had always done in the past. My life had become so confusing. On one hand I could help many people heal themselves but I was finding it a real struggle to heal myself. I retreated again to my inner world and promised myself I wouldn't do any more healing until I had healed myself. I greatly needed to be immersed in the peace of nature.

We took a trip to see our good friends on Anglesey and attended a group meditation at the Roundhouse. I felt comfortable among friends and family just sharing space together. At first we stayed in one of the local B&Bs on the island I hadn't visited before. The owner asked if I would do some healing for his brother who'd recently suffered a stroke and lost the use of his right arm. I couldn't refuse. I just had to help this lovely family so I agreed to see him in one of the spare rooms at the hotel. The images flowed into my mind. My Star Beings were with me while we worked and the session was over in twenty minutes.

It was time to leave to visit my friends on the other side of the island. As we made our way to the car the man who'd had the stroke appeared, rushing over to tell me he had full use of his arm again and had even driven his car that morning, something he hadn't been able to do since his illness. I was really happy for him. So many of these beautiful people had been clients over the years and I knew that healing was my life work. Yet I had to focus on myself now. I felt totally worn out by the one-on-one healing and doing more would just delay my own.

I told James it was time I stopped everything and just rested. We took a holiday caravan in Snowdonia National Park and went into retreat. My health was deteriorating and tests showed a growth in my gall bladder. They were very concerned due to its size and wanted to remove it just to be sure. Instead of accepting surgery, we went to stay in the caravan for the six weeks of James's school summer holiday. We did nothing but rest. I had total faith I would heal and sure enough with James, Mother Nature and my ever-loving guides, my health was completely restored.

After our retreat, I was strong enough to return home and talked with my children by phone. We regained our closeness again. I understood at the time of their father's death they felt they had to lash out at me, the nearest person to them. I also recognized that we have the ability to change moment to moment and that every life experience serves a purpose. We may not understand the purpose when it happens, but over time and on reflection, we can gain real insight and wisdom.

I had a follow-up appointment at Stepping Hill Hospital to see a specialist about the growth. I insisted they do a body scan first to make sure the gall bladder needed removing. The consultant agreed if it would put my mind at rest and I was given an appointment later that week. The day of my appointment, I lay flat on my back while they slid me into a tunnel-like scanner. I had to keep completely still while the device scanned my upper body. The machine made very loud and disturbing noises and the uncomfortable episode lasted about 30 minutes. When the results came back, the hospital staff was surprised to discover there was no trace of a growth. I wasn't a bit surprised since I believed from the start that by dealing with my emotions and resting in nature, I would heal myself.

The infamous year of 2012 prophecy arrived amid much speculation about what it meant and might bring. Though content and taking a rest from full-time healing work, I was aware there was something I needed to do. The idea of writing down my story, which had been simmering for a couple of years started clamoring for attention and wouldn't go away. Even as I wondered at my own audacity, disbelieving that I should even consider the idea, I realised that was the point. There are millions of ordinary people like me who just need to know that we're all extraordinary, and if sharing my journey could help pass that message along to others, my wish would be fulfilled.

Still, I needed someone to help get the tangle of words in my head into an articulate form and asked for the right person to appear. Enter Mel, a former client who became a good friend. Though having moved away many years ago she was also from Stockport and we shared similar memories and experiences. We'd talked then about the possibility of her editing the book but it hadn't been the right time. We'd been out of touch for a while until she rang out of the blue and offered her help so, some months later, here's the book, out in the world at last. Jeff gave me the confidence, Mel made sense of the tangle and I honor them both for their loving support.

In the Stars

"The cosmos is all that is, or ever was, or ever will be."
– Carl Sagan

We are all our own healers. We sometimes need a guide to point us back to ourselves and there are many to choose from, both physical and non-physical, though ultimately we heal ourselves. Everything we seek is within. If we can just become quiet enough to hear our own guidance we will receive the answers we need.

If we blindly trust outer authorities we give away this power, a trust which can literally kill, as when doctors tell a patient they have six weeks to live. If they believe this statement, it's very likely they will die six weeks later. But there are large numbers of people living today because they did not accept that prognosis and used other means to deal with their health challenge.

We have survived on this planet for thousands of years, relying on Mother Nature to sustain us. She will continue to do so only if we wake up and honor her for all she has provided. All of us have everything within us to heal our selves and the Earth. Love yourself and share that love with others and there will be no need for fancy objects that promise you the answer to your healing.

I believe in a loving God, Spirit or divine energy, or whatever you may want to call it and that we are all part of that energy. Some say "God is good with one o". In every case, when I work with people, I call on that constant loving presence that is at the heart of everything. When we reach out to another with a loving heart, anything becomes possible. It's believing and tapping into that infinite field of possibility that makes all the difference.

My experiences have taught me to live my life moment to moment and I look forward to many more years of healing service. Today, I am grateful for everything. I see my children and grandchild regularly. I am so very proud of them and of how they are finding their own way in life. I have my heavenly James by my side, my dearest friends and my greatest teacher to date, my little dog Rosie, although she's no longer in physical form. She passed away peacefully during a recent trip to Wales.

Of all the beings I have been blessed to meet in this life, it was Rosie who demonstrated so clearly the unconditional love that I know to be within each of us. My loving Star Beings are ever on call to faithfully assist in helping whoever appears in my space, whether we're enjoying a delicious cup of tea or performing cosmic brain surgery!

I have always used my imagination and thought 'I can do that,' like a child unrestricted by conditioned restraints. Coming from that child-like place, everything I've wanted has come to pass.

It's in the stars. It's in all I can and cannot see. It's me! And you of course. In the largest sense there is only one of us here!

POSTSCRIPT: THREE HEALING STORIES

Cosmic Brain Surgery

by Jane Hodson

This is the story of an interaction with Julie Bradley, a very special and talented lady who I am delighted to call my friend and confidante. It's a true story...

This is the moment where I tell you that cosmic beings performed brain surgery in my cottage on that very Monday afternoon. I believe this with absolute conviction. If someone had asked me about the possibility of such an occurrence, even just the day before, I would have laughed myself silly. But here's me now, still almost unbelieving, but hand on heart, saying that cosmic brain surgery is what took place that day and this is how it happened:

I reclined back on the massage bed with my eyes shut, while Julie started her work, moving around, without touching me. Somewhere in the realm of consciousness I sensed three 'people' at the head of the bed with one at the foot. He had the air of a supervisor, if you will, watching over the proceedings and making sure that everything was going as planned. I say he, because he looked like a he, much the same as a human, only taller, bigger and bulkier. I don't remember much about the clothing, but I have a sense of some skin showing around the torso. And the head was a slightly different shape – wider at the top, but not domed as you see in 60's sci-fi movies. As I lay there, I heard a voice urging me not to move. Not one muscle.

"You must be very still now, Jane."

There was an energetic presence of hands on my shoulders and holding each side of my head, gently and precisely, helping me stay completely immobile. At the same time, I felt a sensation of a coldness rippling down my body. Not the kind of cold that induces shivers but a different kind of cold altogether, one that held me in a state of quasi-paralysis. I'm not saying that I was unable to move, just that I was capable of holding myself motionless without any effort. Even my breath became so minimal as to negate any visible physical attributes of breathing.

When all was still and motionless, they started performing what can only be described as brain surgery. Long pointed metal instruments were used to probe from the top of my head, deep into its centre. These apparatuses were like elongated knitting needles, but long and fine as if made in titanium or some other perfectly structured metal. Each instrument was used in turn, gently, precisely and silently. There was no pain, no nothing, just the awareness that an extremely delicate procedure was taking place. As a conclusion to the operation, thick, sticky putty was smeared over the wound on the top of my head. Let me say, I'm talking energetically. None of this took place in the physical dimension as we know it.

Clearly, I was somewhat mystified as to what had just occurred but kept my thoughts to myself. Rather than reveal what I had experienced, I was more intrigued to hear what Julie had to say about it all. Without intervention on my behalf, I was curious to know whether our accounts would match and if all that I'd witnessed was imagined or if I'd finally lost the plot.

Once I'd sat up, the first thing Julie said was, "My goodness! You've just had full-on brain surgery!"

"Really?"

She then went onto describe the scene exactly as I had envisioned it. In every detail: the instruments, the sticky yellow poultice and the three 'beings' at the top of the bed, performing the operation.

"Anyone else come to visit that I should know about?"

"Oh yes. There was a supervisor at the foot of the bed, watching over the operation to make sure it went smoothly and according to plan"

OH MY GOD!!

Thankfully it was getting late so I rustled up some supper and shimmied off to bed as quickly as possible. All night long, it seemed as though people were coming in and out of my room, or staying a while to look over me. Julie had talked about the overwhelming love of these beings and how that love had bowled her away.

In my mind's eye, I'd perceived this love as enormous, engulfing waves of emotional bliss. Not so. The love I felt was almost matter-of-fact, an all-embracing love that held neither drama nor attachment, simply because love is all there is. Certainly, these beings were here to help and moved to do so, by and through a love that was unadulterated and true, not mere fodder for the emotions. Does that make sense? I think so.

Before Julie sped off back to the city in her nippy little motor, she urged me to pop back up on the massage bed for a little more work. What happened this time was similar except the atmosphere was more relaxed. No more pointy tools poking around my brain, nor the intense concentration in the air. There was some more fiddling around in my head and then, all of a sudden I felt a clunk deep inside my cranium like you hear about in alien abductions out in the wilds of the American desert as people report getting chipped. Before my imagination went hurtling down that road, it was over and Julie asked me to sit.

"What happened this time, then?" I asked, trying my best not to look quite as freaked out as I was fast becoming.

"Well, I was shown a dial that signifies the balance of your brain. The needle was way over to one side, but with the use of two knobs on either side, I was able to twiddle them to get the needle back to a central position. Once there, I pushed the knobs and the entire apparatus sunk into your brain and into position. I believe that balance is there for good now."

Before I could think about this much longer, Julie had packed down her massage bed and was off. I spent most of that day in the close vicinity of the cottage, moving quietly, being kind to myself, not questioning the course of events too much and grabbing little catnaps as they came my way. Convalescing if you like.

I guess it's all fine and well, indulging in these rites or rituals if that's what you're into. But do they actually make any difference at all? I can't speak with any kind of authority on all the various methods of practice, but with regard this particular episode, I can categorically say, "Yes".

From that day on, I began to notice a pronounced balance of the mind, an increased ability to focus and most of the residual post-accident sketchiness dissipated. Even the egg-sized bump at the crown of my head, that had popped up the night of the Big Bang in London and had never gone away. That went too. Overnight - utterly and completely.

A Need to Share

by Sue

This is a story I never thought I would write. This is my story, a story of recovery and of friendship.

I have been a dedicated and passionately committed nurse for over 30 years. During my professional life I have seen and experienced many things. On a personal level I battled cancer and divorce and successfully managed to be a single parent. I have a beautiful daughter who is my joy. As happens to so many of us, just as life gets to be really good we are thrown yet another challenge. Fortunately, I have been blessed with a positive attitude and believe that the obstacles are there to be overcome. Unfortunately the health problems proved a little more difficult this time.

After several years of cardiac symptoms I consented to cardiac ablation. Unfortunately, there were serious problems during the procedure that left me with a nerve palsy resulting in chronic breathlessness, fatigue and chest pains.

My previously active social and working life were dramatically affected. I had to take medical retirement and gave up my much-loved hobby of dancing. This happened in 2007.

After months of rest, medication, medical tests, hospital visits and consultant advice, I made slow improvement to a point where I could walk short distances but cold and damp conditions affected me badly. Life at this point was very bleak. Many days I was housebound.

A chance remark from a friend made me think about hypnotherapy as a career and my cardiologist agreed it would be a good choice for me. A long search brought me to AHH but health problems kept me from enrolling. Finally I enrolled in September 2008 and met Julie. Very simply, she shines, and I did not know what to make of her. I became engrossed with the course until one day in the spring of 2009. I could never have envisaged what happened.

Julie asked our group, "Who would like a Healing"? I am not the kind of person to take part in such a thing and was shocked when my arm went up of its own accord. What happened next was so profound and life changing that even now I find it hard to understand. My fellow students were observers and equally astounded.

During this time I was seated with my eyes closed. I saw all the major blood vessels in my body, felt my brain move, felt and saw my heart and diaphragm moved back into the correct position.

Afterward, I was exhausted and went home. I spent 3 days in bed. I recovered over the next week. The Peak Flow measurements for my breathing improved radically to the point of being normal.

My second session with Julie proved even more surprising. This time the images were of my skeletal system. I saw a bright light passing through every bone in my body. Again, I was very tired afterward and woke up that night with a burning sensation in my hands. I have osteoarthritis in my hands and other joints. My hands are so improved that I am typing this, something I could not do previously.

My medical consultants are very pleased with my progress. I have gone back to work part-time. I hope to one-day return to my dancing. I am setting up my Hypnotherapy practice and am enjoying life again.

I had lost hope of ever returning to good health. I do not understand Julie's gift but will always be grateful that she shared it with me.

Thank you!

Becoming the Temple of the Heart: An Extraordinary Healer

by Polly

I have always been the kind of person who loves and longs for holy places. It is hard to believe now, but when I was just a little girl I genuinely loved going to our modern Anglican church every Sunday. At that tender age, I didn't enjoy church for any of the reasons I was supposed to, the upbeat liberal sermons that aimed to include the kids and the friendly vicar who asked us to call him by his first name. I didn't even like the explosive hymns that burst into a riot of joyous abandon despite a piano with squeaky pedals and children clutching homemade instruments like they were the bible itself.

Our small church was home to yoga, knitting circles and weekend bingo. It was a tatty place with foldaway chairs and coffee stains up and down the shabby floorboards but to me, at that time, it was nothing less than the gateway to the gods. My very favourite part of Sunday was walking up the path on our small estate to this unlikely temple. Only a child can make such a pilgrimage, in the complete trusting knowledge that there is a place that can be reached, just up that road, where you can truly make your connection with the divine. Long after I stopped loving that church and looked for other hymns to sing, I still found myself making that child-like pilgrimage. I have walked up holy mountains and into wild places looking for the right place, the place where such a connection may be possible. Sometimes, like many other lonely pilgrims, I found what I was looking for, and other times the longing simply tore me from the best side of myself.

So it has been in that way that I have spent a large part of my adult life chasing that connection. Throughout the years of personal development workshops and private practices that have become both my story and my searching itself, I have indeed made progress but have always longed for something like a direct experience of the divine. And it was in that way, armed with nothing but a pilgrim's sympathy, that I began working with one of the world's most extraordinary healers.

When I first met Julie Bradley I was, amongst other things, confused. My heart lay firmly impaled between the reluctant healer I knew I was and the brutal skeptic I felt I should be. Ten years previous experience as a Reiki practitioner had taught me that healing simply could not be dismissed altogether. Evidently my friends and family members loved it because they asked for it often. But any time I began to count on the energies even slightly, trust them, or take them for granted, they became as elusive and transient as the changing sky.

By the time I met Julie in September of last year I had almost entirely given up on the many healers I knew and started an open if slightly scandalous affair with skepticism itself. It didn't take me long to realise that Julie was different from any other healer I had ever met. On the day I was introduced to her, she innocently walked past me in the corridor in the same gentle unassuming way she does everything. Something, a physical and tangible force, nearly knocked me off my feet. At that time I knew Julie was a hypnotherapist and had studied many other disciplines like live blood analysis, but I didn't know she was also a healer. I immediately set about convincing myself that the experience I had just received was something to do with a rather hurried lunch, but little did I know there would be much more to come.

When I first met Julie she had recently returned from a successful trip to California and had many amazing, inspirational stories to share. Her personal journey has brought her into contact with such luminaries as Dr Eric Pearl (The Reconnection,) John of God (Brazil's leading spiritual healer), Professor Ervin Laszlo (scientist and prolific author) and Dr Masuro Emoto (Secret Life of Water) to name just a few.

I have received many healings from Julie, the first of which only lasted about five minutes but later caused me to pass out fully clothed on my unmade bed for about fourteen hours straight. I couldn't even rouse myself to get up and turn off the light. The first thing that happened when she laid her hands on me was that every atom and molecule in my body suddenly started to vibrate, then seemed to stand up and move to the left in a great whizzing motion. If it sounds unnerving, that is because it definitely was, but I was not scared. Even though most of my body was shaking, a larger part of me was, in fact, in complete peace.

Before meeting Julie I would have described myself as the type of person who has never had a psychic experience in their life. This, incidentally, has never bothered me or been a great ambition. However, when I am working with her I see angels, energies and beauty of all kinds. There is something mysterious about this very unassuming woman that seems to turn ordinary people into gifted mystics. I am not alone; her humility, compassion and obvious gifts have gained her a loyal following.

On one occasion I lay down on her soft and comfortable therapy bed, heavy with the usual struggle of trying to live in a world so disconnected from the divine. As she began moving her hands around my body, playing, moving energy around and discarding things no longer needed, I began to drift away. It seemed to me at that moment that the room was abundantly filled with heavenly energy. This was not just a mild notion or an imaginative impression, I quite literally had the physical sensation that the room was filled with light and that many, many individual hands were working on me. The air felt pregnant with an otherworldly sweetness, whilst the sound of music not quite audible to human ears seemed to engulf my senses from every direction. This was both an intensely beautiful experience and a slightly terrifying one. Sometimes when the divine comes to greet you in an everyday place the experience can rock you to the very core of your being, but this explosive movement that can both shape and rebuild you is an absolute blessing.

Julie has used a range of healing techniques with me: hypnotherapy, something akin to spirit surgery, and her extraordinarily powerful energy work. Julie has been able to switch between a range of wonderful skills to achieve breathtaking results, bringing me both closer to my self and the divine in one rapid movement.

She works sincerely and from the heart without ego. Like a child staring into the sacred altar of becoming, Julie appears constantly delighted and enlivened by her work. She has made my world a more magical place and has shown me that it is possible to build a holy place within my own heart.

PHOTOS

Mum, Jack, Grandma and
Julie at Mums wedding

Portwood, Stockport, 1963

Gateway Standing stones,
Anglesey

Witchcraft Museum,
Bostcastle, Cornwall

Jill, Sarjana, Julie. Grand Canyon

John of God, Sarjana and
Julie. Brazil

Rosie and Julie

Pyramid, Egypt

Dr Eric Pearl and Julie. Athens

His Holiness Padmashree
Siddhyog and Julie.

Dr Masaru Emoto, and Julie.
Hamburg

Julie, Crop Circle. Wiltshire

ABOUT JULIE ANN BRADLEY

Julie Ann Bradley was born in Cheshire in 1960. Her childhood was unsettled and often violent, though always anchored by a loving mother and grandmother. Her allies during painful times were  loving inner guides who seemed somehow connected to the night-time stars which brought her solace and also to the UFO she encountered at the tender age of five.

Julie was with her mother and Aunt at the time. The UFO was hovering above her neighbourhood. The encounter did not scare Julie. If anything she was completely fascinated and afterwards, was often seen on her three-wheeler trike peddling like fury down the street where she lived in a bid to launch herself to the stars!

Further encounters with the paranormal coloured Julie's adolescence but it was a severe case of post-natal depression that finally launched her on the quest for answers.

Initially studying Human Biology and Psychology, Julie became a Reiki Master and Hypnotherapist. Julie also qualified in Live Blood Microscopy and Colon Hydrotherapy and trained with Dr Eric Pearl in The Reconnection and Reconnective Healing. She was a co-founder and principal co-ordinator of the Academy of Holistic Hypnotherapy in Manchester, England from 2005-2009.

Her journey as a healer has taken her around the world, meeting along the way some of the authors, scientists and spiritual leaders of today's human potential movement.

There are numerous healing episodes Julie has performed worldwide including working with celebrities.

Julie has performed 'Cosmic Surgery' on a woman with a brain trauma and a woman with a hole in the heart, she has healed herself of a gall bladder complaint and helped a woman overcome schizophrenia.

Although unassuming and grounded, her intuitive healing abilities and deep connection to Source have helped many people make remarkable personal transformations.

She has been requested to speak on the London circuit and in the States on several occasions where she has previously performed healing in Sedona, Arizona and Los Angeles.

You may contact Julie and/or get on her mailing list at: julieannbradley.com

Printed in Great Britain
by Amazon.co.uk, Ltd.,
Marston Gate.